BU

Irish Pub Guide

Recent winners of Bushmills Bar of the Year

- Da Vincis, Londonderry
- Grouse Inn, Ballymena
- Harry's Bar, Banbridge
- Hillside, Hillsborough
- O'Kanes, Randalstown
- The Stables, Groomsport
- Waterfall, Carnlough

The "Bushmills Bar of the Year" is a competition organised annually among the bars in Northern Ireland. The accolade is awarded by a panel of independent judges, under the auspices of Dillon Bass Limited.

The BUSHMILLS Irish Pub Guide

Sybil Taylor

Appletree Press

For Maebeth Fenton
In gratitude for invaluable help, warm friendship, and good times.

Published by
The Appletree Press Ltd
19–21 Alfred Street
Belfast BT2 8DL
1994

A catalogue record for this book is available from the British Library.

ISBN 0 86281 385 9

Cover illustration:
Robert Stewart's Spirit Grocer Drumbeg, by Colin Davidson

9 8 7 6 5 4 3 2 1

CONTENTS

ACKNOWLEDGMENTS

Grateful acknowledgment is made for permission to reprint the following copyright material.

Text of the pamphlet "Beezie" reprinted by permission of Beezie's, Sligo, Co. Sligo.

Excerpts and the poem entitled "Phoenix Park" by Brendan Behan from *Brendan Behan's Island* (London: Hutchinson, 1962, reprinted by permission of Leresche and Sayle. Copyright © Brendan Behan.

Excerpt from "It's Been Copasthetic Here", by James Cameron from *The New Statesman*, August 5, 1966, reprinted by permission of *The New Statesman*.

Excerpts from "The Long Memories of Mayo" by Thomas Flanagan from *Geo* magazine, April 1980, reprinted by permission of Wallace and Sheil Agency, Inc. © Thomas Flanagan, 1980.

Descriptions of Sail Inn and Paddy's Pub in Tipperary courtesy of Hugh Leonard.

Excerpts from the pamphlet "The Bailey, the Story of a Famous Tavern," by Ulick O'Connor, reprinted by permission of The Bailey.

"Raftery the Poet" by Anthony Raftery, translated by Frank O'Connor, from *A Book of Ireland*, edited by Frank O'Connor, reprinted by permission of Fontana Books.

PREFACE

In Ireland the inevitable never happens - the unexpected always.
J.P. Mahaffy

There are about 11,000 pubs in Ireland, and much as I would have enjoyed dawdling about the countryside testing and tasting in everyone of them, it's just not practically possible (still, a person can dream, can't she?). So if you discover a glaring omission, or find that a pub I've included is gone or has changed its name, I'd like to count on you to let me know, and I'll be sure to look into it for the book's next edition.

I count on you because that is actually the way this book was written - listening to recommendations, asking questions, following up on people's enthusiastic loyalties, passionate opinions and pleasant memories. And it was through this rather personal method of researching that I learned that Dublin and Belfast may well be the official capitals of Ireland, but the true centre of Irish life lies in her pubs.

In exploring Ireland's delightful network of these small "community centres", I've tried to include not only a description of the pubs themselves, but a little about the landscape, the food and the people that gives each place its own, special flavour. I hope that I have succeeded and I wish you a safe and happy journey on the pub trail.

To say that my research for this book was a pleasure is an understatement, but without help it just wouldn't have been possible. My thanks therefore to Dr John Daly, the New York dentist with the Irish soul, for his extensive travels and notes. Thanks too, to Simon O'Hanlon, Orla Carey and Ruth Costelloe of the Irish Tourist Board, and to David Boyce, Stephen Doherty, Louise McKeown and Sheelagh Wylie of the Northern Ireland Tourist Board for their wonderful support and advice. For delightful times, and for aid and succour in Dublin, I am grateful to John Kennedy and to Brian Thornberry of Bord Fáilte.

I am also very appreciative of the assistance given me by James Lyndon and Paul Murphy of Aer Lingus.

To Douglas Marshall, my editor, I tip my hat (or perhaps a better metaphor would be raise my glass) in gratitude. He has been the soul of patience, wit and professionalism and I have thoroughly enjoyed working with him.

A number of pals and boon companions have given me their thoughts on the subject of my book, and I'd like to thank John Daly (of Kerry), Bill Cole and John Gore-Grimes for their efforts in setting me on the right path.

LEINSTER

ABBEYLEIX, CO. LAOIS

MORRISSEY'S

Main Street

Morrissey's is an archetypical half-pub, half-shop. The pub has been in the same family since 1775 and has resisted change like a rock in the sea. All the old biscuit bins, tea tins and wooden counters are still in place, and there are great, old-fashioned glass jars full of a mind-boggling variety of scrumptious lollies. Far from being a museum, the shop still does a lively trade with the locals, selling all manner of goods including a special brand of tea packed on the premises.

In the old days, a publican and shop keeper was often also a funeral director, a case of one-stop shopping, so to speak, and Morrissey's has kept up the tradition. Shutters are closed on the days of a funeral, and a horse-drawn hearse is still in operation.

This is a great place for a pint, tea, coffee or a sandwich break on the Dublin-Cork road, and if it's cold, there's even a pot-bellied stove to warm your toes.

ATHLONE, CO. WESTMEATH

Athlone, situated on the Shannon River, is an excellent place for exploring the shores and islands of Lough Ree. This lake, meeting place of counties Westmeath, Roscommon and Longford, is really not a lake at all but the enlarged bed of the river. Several of its many islands harbour the skeletons of ruined churches on their woody shores. The town itself has a pretty marina and a lovely river park with cascades of sky-tinted water to please the eye and heart.

Fourteen miles (22.5 km) east of Athlone on the Mullingar road is the place traditionally known as the "true centre of Ireland," the Hill of Uisneach. Uisneach has been described as the navel of Ireland, and it's no ordinary mound; physically its slopes stretch out over five townlands and historically over many centuries, back into prehistory. Earthworks, ring forts, stones and tumuli are scattered over its surface, creating a deserted village of the ancients.

On the southwest slope is a large natural rock formation called the Catstone because it crouches like a cat watching a mouse. The ancient tribes called it "the Rock of Divisions" because it marked the midland boundaries of the five original provinces.

In later times St Patrick made his bed upon Uisneach, and St Brigid is said to have professed her religion here. She is commemorated by a shrine and a holy well.

SEAN'S

King's Road

Tucked in a narrow street, Sean's is a classic old pub. It is long and narrow with small, scarred wooden tables and a fireplace around which gather the usual assortment of local people. The ceilings are low, the walls smoky, the windows small and dim — in other words, the place is cosy. When I asked the age of the pub, I was told, "Sure and 'tis very old."

On the wall opposite the bar, preserved under a dusty pane of glass, is a bit of wall from one of the crannógs, or ancient, wattle, lake dwellings that housed the ancestors of those drinking here.

At any time in Sean's, someone is likely to break out a guitar and/or other instrument and perform a variety of ballads from pop to traditional. Indeed, Sean's is a kind of clubhouse for the young of Athlone and the farms around it.

BANAGHER, CO. OFFALY

Banagher, on a slope of the east bank of the River Shannon, is a good centre for exploring the western part of the county. There are excellent mooring facilities, and large, deep pools in the river with numerous pike, perch and bream.

HOCKS

A husband and wife team run this pub which is a great hit with the people who tour up and down the Shannon. They've kids galore, and she's a marvellous character, infamous for playing the piano. The pub consists of a great many higgledy piggledy rooms, and while you may be intimidated by the outside, persevere. You can't always tell a pub by its cover, and this one is a must.

Note: Things change slowly at Hock's. A tourist once left a jacket behind, and when he returned a year later, it was still there, exactly where he had left it.

Bettystown, Co. Meath

Meath is rich in history. The book of Kells was created here and that eighth-century marvel, the Tara Brooch, was found in the sands of the beach at Bettystown in 1850.

McDonough's
Here's a good, old thatched pub with a grocery store at one end. After a few pints you might feel like going out to sift the sands and see what you can come up with.

Blackrock, nr Dundalk, Co. Louth

The Brake Tavern
The Brake, a seafront pub, is a wonderful place for either a pint, a cup of tea or a delicious variety of things to eat, from seafood (speciality of the house) to steak. Its wooden interior is full of comfortable, country furniture and a museumload of local memorabilia. An open fire invites the visitor to pull up a chair and sit for a while.

Booterstown, Co. Dublin

Gleason's
This very popular pub has been going for years. The bar is traditional, but the pub has a "sitting room" type of atmosphere complete with armchairs.

Wry comment from a "thirty something," devotee: "All the pubs we go to have to have armchairs now, because the young crowd is all ageing." Actually, the generational profile of Ireland does show that the majority of the population is now in the "thirty something" category. So pub owners take note—armchairs, not stools.

Carlingford, Co. Louth

The town of Carlingford is on the southern shore of Carlingford Lough at the foot of Slieve Foye. The ubiquitous St Patrick is said to have landed here on his return from Rome, harkening to a voice in a dream that bid him return to a land where he once tended sheep for a Druid master.

At one time this strategic harbour (used by early Norse raiders to plunder the hinterlands) had no less than thirty two castellated buildings defending it. In today's Carlingford, you can see the massive sixteenth-century ruin of King John's castle, or the large square of Taaffe's Castle (near Newry Street), with its wonderful spiral staircase leading to the battlements.

P.J. O'Hare's Anchor Bar

This very small pub and grocery store combination is full of character. In the family since 1860, the pub is owned by Mr P.J. O'Hare himself, who keeps an open fire going in the pleasant little lounge decorated with pub mirrors and curios.

Try the local oysters here, they are a special treat, although the home-made brown bread, smoked salmon, soup and sandwiches are also good. On fine days, move the feast outdoors to a pleasant white-washed enclosed yard with simple seating made of barrels.

Castledermot, Co. Kildare

Doyle's

You wouldn't necessarily notice Doyle's on the Carlow-Kilkenny road, but it's one of those little pubs that is a true gem. Small, simple, and clean. Wooden stools and tables, an open fire, no television, good conversation. It's a favourite stopping point for everyone in the area.

Clane, Co. Kildare

Jones'

Virtually all the pubs in Clane, a pretty village in the heart of horse country, feature paintings or photographs of equine luminaries, but this pub is special. It is owned by Nick Cash, himself a celebrated show jumper, and in the pleasant and light back room there are photos of him starring in various events. The little bar out front is almost as small as a snug.

Note: Don't miss the Clane hairdresser's shop. A one-room cottage of ancient and moss covered stone, it looks as though you'd get a haircut by elves or trolls in there.

Manzor's

This building dates back to 1730 but there's been a pub here for the last century. The Manzor family have owned it since 1936, and Seamus Manzor, the barman, is a good man to have behind the imbibing counter. He's willing to stop and have a chat any time. Rumour has it that one of the Rolling Stones comes in here for the odd pint. Who knows, if you're a fan maybe you'll get lucky. A spacious back room, sandwiches, tea and coffee.

Coolrain, Co. Laois

From the plain that forms most of this county rise the lovely Slieve Bloom Mountains in the northwest, a surprise to those who think of Laois mainly as a road connecting Dublin, Cork and Limerick.

Sheehan's

This old-time pub offers a log fire all year around and tables made of tree trunks. At closing time the proprietress has been known to deal with those who endlessly procrastinate by chasing them out with a broom, a process which everyone seems to enjoy.

Dalkey, Co. Dublin

Dalkey, a fashionable suburb of Dublin, is a picturesque village about eight miles (13 km) from Dublin's centre. It can be easily reached by train or bus. If you're driving, you'll be taking the beautiful "Rocky Road To Dublin" celebrated in the song.

Finnegan's/The Sorrento Lounge

Take the Dart commuter train and enter the first pub you meet within a hundred yards of the Dalkey station. Nice homely atmosphere. Nice publican.

The Queen's

12 Castle Street

The feeling in this good size pub, done in pine and shades of antique yellow and terra-cotta, is fresh as the nearby sea. The Queen's has repeatedly and deservedly won awards for décor, professionalism, good food and drink and a staff who perfectly balance friendliness and efficiency. Try their chilli con carne.

Bar Food 12 noon–6 p.m.

Donadea, Co. Kildare

Roche's

Finding Roche's in the first place is half the fun. I'm not even going to attempt to give you directions—suffice it to say that the pub is at the back of beyond of Donadea, which in itself is not exactly a busy metropolis. The best thing to do is to get to Donadea and ask directions.

Asking the way is rather like going on a treasure hunt, and the directions themselves often have a mythical quality. Sample: "Turn left at the crossroads with the big, auld dead tree, pass the field with the great stone in the middle, then a sharp right onto the forest road. You'll think you're on the wrong road because the holes are that bad, but it's about three miles in—sure, you can't miss it."

I'm here to tell you that you can, but there are worse thing to do than to drive around the beautiful Kildare countryside at sunset looking for a pub.

Don't be alarmed when you do finally reach your goal. Roche's looks like something out of a fairy-tale, a kind of tumbledown witch's house full of ancient spells. In this case, it belongs to someone who in fact *is* rather like the Good Witch of the North.

I met Mrs Roche shortly after entering her domain, stooping through a low door to find myself in a bare-bones, yet strangely cosy environment. There were three rooms with turf fires and plain wooden tables and chairs. The ancient stone floor rose and fell unevenly, and in the main room a ramshackle bar ran along one wall, while the seating along the other was reminiscent of the back seats of cars.

And here it was that I found the eighty-year-old Mrs Roche, in every way a lady, impeccably dressed in a navy blue suit with a string of pearls at her neck, and the accents of her British childhood upon her lips. She was the soul of graciousness, bringing me tea and biscuits beside the fire and chatting until I felt a sense of well-being, peace and comfort that had evaded me in many a more fancy bar.

Mrs Roche, now a widow, came to Ireland from London during World War II, married a Dubliner and bought the place in 1953 from a family who had owned it since 1780. "I was raising kids then," she told me,"everyone thought we were mad. There wasn't even electricity then, but I liked the country. I thought it was wonderful. It wasn't easy, though, my husband had a stroke and was in hospital for six years."

As we talked her great-grandchildren, curious about the guest from New York, kept appearing from the family quarters out back. One wanted to play me his tin whistle, another announced that she had received Honours in maths. "They'll be going to Trinity some day," Mrs Roche said fondly.

Roche's and its charming owner have become a kind of underground legend among people who appreciate this kind of a rough, country pub. If it sounds like your sort of a place too, you'd better hurry out there and find it, because Mrs Roche is talking of selling.

"They'll fix the place up," she said, "in a way I never could afford. And then it will be beautiful."

Dublin City

Dublin is the great mother of all Irish pubs (there are well over a thousand pubs in the city). You can almost believe the town was invented as an excuse for their creation. There is a pub for every occasion from a funeral to a dart contest, and for every kind of patron, from barrister to fisherman. And then there are those pubs that mix all these elements together. A word of warning: if you are visiting Dublin it is possible to enjoy pub crawling so much that you endlessly postpone departure.

As you wander through Dublin, you'll find Ireland's history present in the names of the streets and the numerous statues. Justly known as the largest village in the world, Dublin's structure is organic rather than mechanical. Her people, buildings, streets and pubs are living history, like the rings of a tree. In a sense, Dublin's appeal resides in the fact that it is still a town on the human scale.

People can and do know one another well; they greet one another in the streets and pubs. Human beings are not dwarfed by high rises or their own creations.

In the deep tranquillity of St Stephen's Green, the park made famous by James Joyce, time slows as you watch the swans in the lake and the strolling students from nearby Trinity College. It is easy to enter the rhythm of a bygone era, to feel the ghosts of the great Irish writers whose ambiençe now surrounds you: Shaw and Yeats, Joyce and Wilde, Sheridan and O'Casey, Behan and Beckett.

Here in this town, where so much legend is concentrated, where the famous and often lethal Irish combination of drink and talk has flowered into great literature and enduring wit, it is easy to wax romantic. But the Dubliner will not let you get carried away for long. "In Ireland," as Sean O'Faolain said, "it is bad taste to be serious." And the Dubliner would agree.

The Bailey

2–3 Duke Street

A short history of The Bailey provides the best possible starting point from which to view Irish life and Irish personalities—literary, social, and political.

The Bailey began modestly enough as an eating house in 1837. Gradually it became a meeting place for the brightest minds and wits of Ireland until, at the turn of the century, it had turned into a kind of super-pub, the ideal of Irish pubdom. The pronouncements and quips delivered over a pint at The Bailey would soon be repeated all over Dublin. "They would sacrifice their own mother for a witty phrase," is how one contemporary described it.

Ulick O'Connor, the well-known writer, has compared The Bailey in its heyday to The Mermaid Tavern of Elizabethan England:

> The Bailey has points of comparison with The Mermaid Tavern, the reputation of a heady phrase on the general mouth, the recitation of a verse casually composed about some current event . . . In those years, the pace of life in Dublin left plenty of room for tongue-wagging. Any event of note in the city was sure to unleash its chain of anecdotes and be embroidered by the wits and raconteurs as soon as it reached their eager ears.
>
> At The Bailey, the passion that Dubliners have for clinical observation and exploration of character was given full reign.

> Local personalities were incorporated into anecdotes, illustrative of their personal idiosyncrasies or eccentricities. It did not matter if the tales concerned friends of the group discussing them. The artist's licence was allowed to the teller of the tale.

The hub around which the Bailey group revolved was Arthur Griffith. He was the founder of Sinn Féin (Ourselves Alone), which from 1906 advocated a separate parliament and a massive programme of industrialisation. Along with two or three others, Arthur Griffith created the basis of the modern Irish state. Most of the writers of the Irish literary renaissance—W.B. Yeats, Padraic Colum, James Stephens, et al.—wrote for Griffith's newspaper, *The United Irishman.*

Though Churchill noted that Griffith was "that unusual figure, a silent Irishman," Griffith was a good listener and created a climate in which wit and conversation thrived. He was also an accomplished balladeer, and on special occasions would sing his "Ballad of the Thirteenth Lock," a song about a haunted bargeman which is frequently sung today but which few know was composed by Griffith.

The upstairs room where Griffith held sway (now a restaurant) has a history as an unofficial centre for political as well as literary ferment. Tradition has it that Parnell and members of the Irish Party came here, and that it was also a meeting place used by the secret revolutionary group, The Invincibles.

Michael Collins, the legendary IRA general, came to The Bailey when he was on the run from the Black and Tans, a special force of British ex-servicemen so called because of their mixed police-and-military uniform. Collins visited The Bailey and went straight upstairs because of the presence of the British military in the bar in the evenings.

Since it attracted a literary set, there are many references to The Bailey in works by well-known writers. James Stephens, author of *The Crock of Gold*, a tale of philosophy and leprechauns, remembers his first visit there:

> Upon an evening I found myself in The Bailey in front of a drink. I had my first adventure in the air, oxygen and gin, which we call wit, and which I watched as a cat watches a mouse, meaning to catch it, and for the first time I heard poetry spoken of with the assured carelessness with which a carpenter talks of his planks and of the chairs and tables and oddments he will make with them.

Oliver St John Gogarty, the writer, surgeon, airman and famed conversationalist, remembered The Bailey as "The Museum of Dublin because it houses the Muses."

It was also the house of the individual. Colourful characters abounded, my favourite being Valentine Nolan-Whelan. Valentine was a barrister and bon vivant. Twice he broke the bank at Monte Carlo. He liked to buy unusual underwear for his girlfriends, but this could not have been the reason he was constantly broke, as he had, aside from his earnings at the casino and race courses, a considerable private income. When he did finally go broke, he did it with style: while entertaining at dinner he enjoined the butler at each course to "make sure the boys are well fed." Who were the boys? The bailiffs who were at that moment removing the furniture from some of the other rooms.

With the death of The Bailey's owner, William Hogan, in 1945, the pub became more of a fashionable eating house, catering to international names such as Margot Fonteyn, Charlie Chaplin, Peter Ustinov and Evelyn Waugh.

I will now practise the colourful gambit of the "aside," a technique frequently encountered in the labyrinthine conventions of Irish conversation. Speaking of Evelyn Waugh, Brendan Behan tells a great pub story in *Brendan Behan's Island—An Irish Sketchbook*: "There's a pub up near Guinness's Brewery on the Liffey Quay. . . The Shaky Man. I don't know if it's there now, it's been a long time since I was in it, but I think it was there I heard one of my friends—a man named Crippen—refer to Evelyn Warr. 'Aye,' he said, 'Evelyn Warr was a tough woman . . . and,' says he, 'she was a great soldier and a great warrior. And she was called Evelyn because that was her name and she was called Warr because she was all for war.'"

And speaking of Brendan Behan (now I'm going to get back to the original subject without skipping a beat, a skill also acquired in Dublin pubs), he too was a frequent imbiber at The Bailey, part of the literary crowd that was to reappear under the aegis of John Ryan, who owned the pub from 1958 to 1971. John Ryan, himself an artist and man of letters, created the ambience that drew the likes of Miles Na Gopaleen, J.P. Donleavy and Patrick Kavanagh.

But The Bailey's most famous literary patron was probably James Joyce, and the pub is now the repository for a fine piece of Joyceina, a blue door marked with the number 7. This is the actual door from number 7 Eccles St immortalised by Joyce as the house of Leopold Bloom in *Ulysses*. The house was in fact the home of his friend John

Francis Byrne, who was to become Crawley in *Portrait of the Artist as a Young Man*. (It was demolished in 1967). Other literary and historical memorabilia abound.

Though these days the pub is a busy lunchtime and after-work favourite for business types, bankers and lawyers, sometimes among the voices and the laughter, I seem to hear a ghostly, ironic chuckle and I'll take bets on who it is.

The Bleeding Horse/The Falcon

24 Camden Street Upper

This was originally a halting spot for coaches on the way to Rathmines. Back in 1649 Cromwell's men defeated the royalists at the battle of Rathmines, and one tradition has it that after the battle, the wounded horses were rounded up and doctored at the old pub which stood in the middle of the highway here. At that time, it was thatched and surrounded by fields.

The present building is a nineteenth century replacement of a timber faced inn which was built here in 1710, from which date The Bleeding Horse name first appears. Another apocryphal story is that when coach horses suffered from "head staggers," they were bled here by a farrier. The old sign over the door showed a bleeding white stallion being attended.

People still refer to the pub by its old name, although in 1960 the new owner changed it to The Falcon Inn, because, as one story goes, he was not enamoured of Dubliners' often colourful delivery of the word "bleedin'".

Take this with a pinch of salt and stop off here to recall a Camden street that echoed to the clatter of hoofbeats and the jingle of harnesses as the post-chaises and stage-coaches came and went. The pints are excellent and the food, though simple, is really good fare, especially the soups, a variety of closed and open sandwiches, and the home-made desserts.

Décor: massive dark timbers and high ceilings which create an atmosphere almost like a medieval hall, gallery seating overlooking the two bars, and a huge fireplace in the smaller bar. Even the loos here deserve commendation—they are exceptionally clean and modern.

Bowes

31 Fleet Street

This is the hang-out for the newspaper crowd, being especially handy for those who labour for *The Irish Times*, whose offices are just a few doors away. This warmly lit pub, with its dark coffered walls and photos of Dublin, is a good place for creative eaves-dropping. In the front are two snugs with milk glass walls from which come periodic bursts of laughter.

Since Ireland is supposed to represent the apogee of the written and spoken word, it is not surprising that a stupendous amount of verbiage pours off the printing presses and into books and magazines, and that newspapers are a very important part of Irish life.

Each province (Ulster, Leinster, Munster and Connacht) has its own paper, published at least once a week, and there is a long list of weekly provincial newspapers too.

THE BRAZEN HEAD

20 Lower Bridge Street

Here we have Dublin's oldest drinking establishment. The Brazen Head was formally chartered in 1688, but a place of refreshment for the weary traveller has existed on this spot probably since the twelfth century. The present building was a coaching inn erected circa 1700, and an advertisement in a Dublin paper of 1750 reads, "Christopher Quinn of the sign of The Brazen Head in Bridge Street, being determined to continue the wine trade as usual, has fitted said house with neat accommodations and commodious cellars for said business." The landing window still contains early bottle glass and one pane bears a nice bit of scratched graffiti: "John Langan halted here, 7th August, 1726."

As soon as you enter the crooked door (or is it the building that defies gravity?) you will find yourself plunged into an alluring warren of nooks, crannies and passageways that fairly breath history. The lighting is suitably dim and smoky (there are fireplaces in every room) and the low-ceilinged front room with its corner bar invites the exchanging of confidences.

Certainly, historic secrets and confidences were once the order of the day here: in 1798 and the years immediately prior to that, the chiefs of the United Irishmen used to meet and relax at the Brazen Head. At times, the pub was frequented by Robert Emmet, Wolfe Tone and Daniel O'Connell as well as many other notables. Robert Emmet actually lived here for a while, renting a room that overlooked the passageway leading to the door of the inn, and from where all callers to the house could be observed. Ask to see the desk he used for his writings, just one of the wonderful antique treasures that you'll find here.

The back room serves a fine lunch of the Chef's hot specials plus a carvery, and there's traditional music in the music room every night except Thursday (Jazz and Blues on Thursdays).

Brian Boru House/Hedigan's

5 Prospect Road, Glasnevin

The Brian Boru is on the road to Glasnevin Cemetery, and has long been a popular stop for funeral cortèges, serving as a kind of decompression chamber between the grief of the burial and the return home to Dublin.

James Joyce records the route of such a procession in *Ulysses*, and Brendan Behan records a marvellous cameo of two drunks in the famous cemetery.

> They asked for Mulcahy of the Coombe and were told where he was buried. After traipsing through the fog, they found the grave, sure enough. One of the drunks spelt out the name: Terrence Mulcahy. The other drunk was blinking up at the statue of Our Saviour the widow had put up. "Not a bloody bit like the man," says he, "That's not Mulcahy," says he, "whoever done it."

But people don't flock to The Brian Boru, or Hedigan's as it is more commonly known, simply to drown their sorrows. It is one of the most famous of Dublin's northside pubs, hugely popular with the residents of the neighbourhood and with the crowds from

Dalymount Park, as well as with the passing trade. Lots of local wit and banter here, in a house well run and with a long tradition of top class refreshments and comfort. There's a beautiful conservatory and garden in the back, and you can drive there secure in the knowledge that there's plenty of room for your car in the spacious car park.

CAFÉ EN SEINE

40 Dawson Street

The O'Dwyer family run many of Dublin's pubs, but this one is their current flagship. The En Seine, fondly nicknamed "the insane," by cognoscente, is a trend setter, Dublin's first attempt at a pub-cum-café, combining the traditions of Paris and those of Dublin.

There's no sign out for the En Seine, but look for it across the street from the Lord Mayor's Mansion. This pub is, as a Dublin friend told me, "very, very 'in' and trendy," and unique in Dublin in that the front of the pub is set aside for those customers who want to sip caffeine and eat pastries.

The En Seine is the place if you want to have a night out in a pub, but you don't particularly want to drink (more and more the case for Dubliners). Here you can settle yourself in the café area with a cappuccino, and watch all the beautiful people getting drunk.

The décor is stunning and as avant garde as the concept. A vaulted, cathedral ceiling painted with stylised Celtic themes, arches above brick walls. The general colours are peach and turquoise, in a kind of tasteful "Book of Kells meets Art Deco" style, if you can imagine that.

There's a wonderful balcony, rather like a choir loft, from where you can survey the people below thronging the endlessly long, brass-topped bar lit by milk globed chandeliers. There are couches up here for private tête-à-têtes, and you'll notice that even the loo doors have stained-glass art deco panels.

In the back bar lounge, the ceiling is draped in filmy white cloth and white neoclassic columns rise from the bar to the ceiling in a style that verges delightfully on the camp.

The café area is of course plastered with one whole wall section of "Toujours Ricard" apéritif posters. The café menu features café au lait, cappuccino, expresso, double expresso, expresso Romano, pastries, patisseries and tartes, a selection of breads and rolls, a variety of cheeses, wines from Portugal, Italy, France and Spain, French champagne, apéritifs, pastis, Pernod, Kir and Kir Royal. Music is intermittently and appropriately French—Piaf and company.

I say vive the En Seine.

CONNOLLY'S/THE SHEDS

198 Clontarf Road

The Sheds is a wonderfully friendly, calm, old-fashioned pub just meant for conversation or reading or just dreaming away a few tranquil hours. The pub is located on the waterfront road to Howth and gets its name from the days when fishermen had their sheds here to dry their nets. On the walls are numerous prints of these old sheds as well as photos of tram sheds which also played an important role in Dublin history. Trams were a big part of community life when Dublin was a smaller city and the suburbs were little villages around it—satellites like Clontarf, Rathmines, Dun Laoghaire and Sandymount.

The tram sheds were just up the road and in one photo taken in the 1920s you can see Connolly's façade and the glass globes of the gas lamps. The façade has changed very little since present owner Peter Connolly, was born in a room above the pub (now a lounge—the family has moved next door). Peter's father bought the pub in 1927, and when Peter inherited it in 1962, he was very gentle with the modernising process.

"We had an old clock that was lying out in the back for thirty years," he says. "It had been over the bar for sixty years before that, and so when we renovated the place and brought it back to its old look, we put the clock up again. Lucky we kept it."

Connolly's is a true "local" in the best sense.

"Ah sure you know the parents and the grandparents," Peter says, smiling his kind smile. "It's funny, the drinkin' pattern of people. Like you could get the grandfather but his son won't come in. But the next generation after that does come in—the father wouldn't be drinkin' with the son, but the grandson will come in. People come here because they know they're looked after. Also we don't shove the price up either."

The front bar room is extremely comfortable, with muted though fresh colours and an aura of authenticity that avoids the trendily quaint. The crowd in the front is mixed local and commuter, and for the young there's a back lounge for playing cards at red and green tiled tables under banners of American football and baseball teams.

DAVY BYRNE'S

21 Duke Street

"He entered Davy Byrne's. Moral pub." So James Joyce refers to Davy Byrne's in *Ulysses*. Entering it yourself, you may still get a feel for what was meant by that slightly enigmatic description. Although the pub has undergone major changes since Joyce immortalised it, it remains a friendly and excellent place to catch the modern version of Joyce's "Dubliners" at play. Situated on Duke Street, off Dawson Street, the pub is in the exact centre of the city—a convenient meeting place.

There are three bars, each with a separate entrance: the main bar, the Ulysses Bar and the main lounge which used to be the famous "back room." Though the place has been unassertively modernised, some links with the old days remain. In the Ulysses Bar is a remarkable engraved mirror showing the upper yard of Dublin Castle in 1880. With bottles and glasses standing before it, the effect is interestingly surreal, particularly if you are under the influence of one of Davy Byrne's "specials."

In the main bar are some captivating murals, the work of Brendan Behan's father-in-law, Cecil French Salkheld. One, of a 1940s bucolic bacchanal in the idyllic Irish countryside, includes a portrait of a nattily attired Davy Byrne sitting under a tree. His expression, that of a slightly bemused, interested bystander thoughtfully surveying the whole scene, must certainly have been drawn from life.

DOHENY & NESBITT

5 Lower Baggot Street

This pub is probably one of the most popular in Dublin for all generations. After you've seen its perfect antique frontage and the polished brass sign advertising TEA AND WINE MERCHANT, it will come as no surprise to you that the pub is 130 years old and carrying its age beautifully, thank you!

I'm pleased to report that the interior completely lives up to the exterior, a happy harmony that isn't all that common in life. Pass through the swinging doors and you'll find yourself in authentic early Victorian surroundings complete with high ceilings, old whiskey casks, pumps and tankards, wooden partitions, marble

topped tables and antique mirrors. The wooden partitions serve to create intimate islands in the impressive sea of people of all sorts.

At night, both front and back rooms are pretty "packed out" and the barmen are studies in the fine art of skilful bartending under pressure.

I was first introduced to Doheny & Nesbitt during the day, when like most Dublin pubs and people, it offers an entirely different face. The feeling is lazy and easy, the barman is tending to maintenance, polishing this and that, and there is time and peace for artful conversation.

I went there one morning with one of the finest non-stop raconteurs in Ireland, the admirable writer and chronicler, Benedict Kiely. He can blend one story into another as effortlessly as one pint flows into the next.

After a while an American journalist wandered in. He had come to Dublin on a vacation fifteen years earlier and was still there. Immediately the two men became enmeshed in a discussion of Irish historical minutiae that left me miles behind. The journalist departed and with just a pause for a sip, Ben flowed easily into the next story.

> I do remember the pint-drinkers' club in a certain back room. For initiation you had to drink seventeen pints, one after the other, and then buy a round for everyone in sight. The rules were framed on the wall. Membership was naturally exclusive.
>
> Opening off the back room was a sort of hallway with a blind stairway roofed over to make a larger room above. The great joke was to send a half tipsy stranger there looking for the Gents

and then listen attentively for the thump as he ascended the truncated stairway on the road to nowhere and his head made contact with the ceiling and he came reeling out again. I was a victim once. The echoes of laughter are with me still.

The Guinness Hop Store and Brewery Visitors' Bar

Crane Lane off Thomas Street

There's a rich burnt coffee smell which hangs over the Liberties. It's an aroma which haunts the homesick émigré and which comes from a much loved liquid integral to the Irish way of life. The pint. Find out everything you ever wanted to know about the black stuff and more at the Guinness Hop Store and Brewery, and then test the theory that the nearer to the brewery the pub is, the finer its pint, by trying one in the Visitors' Bar. Also available here is a nifty array of Guinness-related clothing and objects. My own favourite items on sale are the witty Guinness advertising posters of the 1950s.

Hours: 10 a.m.–4 p.m., weekdays. Admission charge.

The Hole in the Wall

The Phoenix Park
South Gate

The Hole In The Wall is a bit more elegant than the picture conjured up by its name. It's a long series of connecting rooms comfortably appointed in traditional-modern but not objectionable style—a pleasant place. It has a history of being a traditional "coach-house" and the owners are justifiably proud of it, as you can see from the carpet with the date of establishment woven into it—1610.

Carvery lunch Monday-Friday. Traditional ballads Sunday from 12.30 p.m. Ample parking.

One of the best things about this pub is it its location—smack against the wall of the Phoenix Park. (For some reason, Dubliners never refer simply to Phoenix Park, it's always *the* Phoenix Park).

The Phoenix Park is one of Dublin's great treasures and not to be missed. Less than two miles from the centre of the city, it is very popular both winter and summer. Several dignitaries are fortunate enough to make their headquarters here: the President of Ireland, the Papal Nuncio and the American ambassador have as a common front yard the park's 1,700 acres (688 ha) of pure verdant delight.

The park's meadows and forests have also served Dubliners as garden and playground since 1747, when the Royal Deer Park was thrown open to the public by the Earl of Chesterfield, viceroy at the time. Through the lush green centre of the park runs a magnificent three-mile drive bordered by fine chestnut trees, majestic oaks and groves of hawthorn and silvery birches. If you're lucky, you'll catch a glimpse of the herd of deer that browse in the field beside the road.

Next to the drive is a column bearing a sculpted phoenix, the miraculous bird that rises reborn from its own ashes. The Phoenix Park was named after this bird through a kind of slip of the tongue: "phoenix" is what emerged from the Gaelic "fionn uisce," which actually means "clear water." The water referred to a mineral spring near the north end of the Zoological Gardens.

The Zoological Gardens are "grand" from the first moment you enter, which you do through a whimsical thatched gatehouse, the epitome of all gatehouses built, or rather invented, in 1833. The zoo opened in 1831, which makes it the oldest in the world after London and Paris. There have been considerable changes since then, when the only resident was a wild boar. Now, all the usual denizens of zoos are there, living in exquisitely landscaped gardens surrounding a mirror-smooth pond. Just to add a finishing touch, colourful flamingos and peacocks wander around like living jewels in the leafy green.

HUGHES'S

19 Chancery Street

Hughes's is a market pub and has been so for over a century. Here in the seventeenth century was the Ormond Market which was swept away about 80 years ago, when there were about ten drink outlets in the vicinity. The pub is located at the intersection of St Michan's Place, which, given the plethora of back streets called after the saint, is much less colourful than its original name of Bull Lane.

In medieval times, Chancery Street was called Pill Lane for the Peel or Pool formed here by the Liffey as it lapped against the walls of the great Cistercian foundation of St Mary's Abbey. You can still visit the Chapter House where Silken Thomas threw down the Sword of State in open defiance of Henry VIII.

Michael Hughes's has come to the fore in recent years for the range and quality of traditional musicians who are to be found here nightly. If you are interested in Irish traditional music you are sure of a session here equal to the best on offer anywhere in the city—

and it's free. You can dance a Kerry set here (usually twice a week) but check the evening papers to make sure. A wide variety of international musicians also demonstrate their own particular traditions regularly, be they American, British or Scottish.

The International Bar

23 Wicklow Street

Like many Dublin pubs, this one is situated on a corner, probably so you can be trapped both coming and going. It is a time capsule of the nineteenth century, which is not surprising since the pub has been owned and operated by the same family, the Donohoes, since 1888.

The high ceilings, the massive marble-topped bar and mahogany bar furniture, the brass rails, plants and endless mirrors give a sense of opulent ease; the mysterious caryatides along the main mirror are fun and a nice reminder of Old World classicism. The host is very friendly and doesn't mind sharing his stories and information. The pint pulled here is reputed to be excellent, the crowd youngish and fashionable.

There is a pleasant cellar downstairs.

Kavanagh's

1 Prospect Square
Glasnevin

Next to the back gate of Glasnevin Cemetery is Kavanagh's, in business since 1833 and still owned by the Kavanagh family. The pub is one of the best preserved examples of the "traditional" Irish pub, untouched by that faint whiff of the museum that a restored pub sometimes gives off. Though it has been used as a favourite location for pub shots in many films, it is a real honest-to-God working pub, as attested by the sawdust and unyielding light, and the swinging doors isolating you cosily in your worn wooden snug. The long main room doesn't seem as large as it actually is, since it's partitioned into a variety of cubbyholes and lurking places for comradely drinking and talk.

Around ten in the evening, the place is buzzing, but not uncomfortably packed. The crowd is composed of all ages and occupations.

Kavanagh's connection to Glasnevin Cemetery is more than just proximity—the pub actually has a small opening in one of the walls adjoining the cemetery grounds through which it was customary for thirsty gravediggers to pass a shovel. A pint was placed on the shovel and the work went on, much enlivened.

Most people call Dublin's main cemetery Glasnevin after the suburb it's located in, and they probably wouldn't know what you were talking about if you called it Prospect Cemetery, its real name. But by either name, it is the quintessential graveyard, ideal for a ruminative, elegiac wander among its dark cypress trees and melancholy yews, its angels, pillars, crosses and vaults. (If you want to ramble further among flowers and trees, next door are the Botanic Gardens).

Many of Ireland's illustrious names lie buried here: Michael Collins, Eamon De Valera, Jeremiah O'Donovan Rossa. As you enter the main gate, you'll see a full-sized replica of an ancient Irish round tower, a monument to Daniel O'Connell, dynamic statesman and persuasive orator, and the first Irishman to sit in an English parliament.

A short distance away is a large granite boulder with a giant PARNELL chiselled on it, for though Charles Stewart Parnell was a Protestant, he was granted burial in this Catholic cemetery.

Maybe, as you stroll through this stone garden, you'll hear a mocking laugh, the ghostly mirth of Brendan Behan who lies here finally at rest; and oh yes, the not to be forgotten Barry Fitzgerald, who began his career at the famous Abbey Theatre. I have nothing against the man, but I've yet to hear a single Irishman actually say "top of the mornin' to ya." But then, those were other days and other ways.

Kiely's/Ciss Madden's

22 Donnybrook Road

A large, excellent, new pub with a fin de siècle atmosphere. Art nouveau decorative themes include curlicue mirror trims, traditional mahogany tables on curvaceous wrought-iron bases, stained-glass windows and a clubby snug the size of a small sitting room.

For a totally different experience, go to the back where you'll find Ciss Madden's, also with its own separate street entrance. It's a very traditional, old Dublin spit-and-sawdust kind of place.

Good bar food.

Kitty O'Shea's

25 Grand Canal Street

A glorious example of the resurrection of a once ordinary Dublin pub. Kitty O'Shea's (once Smyth's) is, at this writing, one of the most popular meeting places in the city. Dark wood, snugs, cool stone floors and warm lighting work together to create a friendly feeling, augmented by the pleasant staff. A wide selection of hot and cold lunchtime dishes can be chosen from an appetising buffet.

The pub, named after the woman for whose illicit love Charles Stuart Parnell lost the leadership of the Home Rule party in 1890, is a "must" in any itinerary of the city hostelries.

Live traditional music nightly. Jazz brunch on Sundays.

THE LORD EDWARD TAVERN

23 Christ Church Place

Built by the present owner's grandfather a hundred years ago, the tavern stands on the site of previous taverns dating back to the Middle Ages. It is in the oldest part of the "walled city," a short step from several historic spots—Christ Church Cathedral, St Patrick's Cathedral and Dublin Castle.

The Lord Edward can be enjoyed literally on several levels: on the ground floor is a fine Dublin pub of character; the first floor bar specialises in excellent pub food; the second floor is the place for quality meals of fresh fish, smoked salmon and Dublin Bay prawns.

Closed Sundays.

LYNCH'S/ P. O'LOINSIGH

144 Thomas Street

This small pub is one of the few in Dublin that displays its name in Gaelic over the door. It's a perfect place to visit after you've enjoyed the fabulous multimedia Guinness history show at the Guinness Brewery across the street at St James' Gate.

Lynch's is steeped in history, and present barman Joe Lynch, the seventh generation in this publican family to pull the pints, is glad to tell you all about it.

The pub passed into the hands of Patrick Lynch by the 1860s and rapidly became a hotbed of Fenian activity. On the walls are all manner of patriotic etchings of those days and of the heroes of earlier uprisings as well. Above the bar is the original clock with Patrick Lynch's name spelled out beneath its face. It still works perfectly.

When I stopped in for a simple but satisfying lunch of sandwiches and salad, the clientele was a mixed group—locals, Guinness reps, tourists and office workers. It's one of those intimate, friendly pubs full of easy laughter where a stranger quickly feels welcome.

Joe on the subject of his pub: "The pub dates back to the 1600s and was called the White Bull Inn back then. The crowd that were the first ones drinking here were up from Wexford. In the 1916 days it was known as the gunman's pub because of all the meetings held here and in the neighbourhood.

The Guinness boats docked in this area so it was colourful and crowded for a while, then became very quiet. Now people are moving back because the district is going up-market.

Thirty or forty years ago at Christmas, we'd have hams for sale the whole length of the counter and fellas would just be picking them up as fast as they could. There used to be a barracks here 70 years ago, and a lot of soldiers used to drink here. And the old Stephen's hospital was nearby. We'd get a complete cross-section of characters coming in—the labouring Guinness men and the Guinness management both—as well as the fellas off the boats coming in to get paid.

We still get a good crowd, even now."

McDaid's

3 Harry Street

Say McDaid's and people will answer Brendan Behan. Although the roistering writer is associated with practically every pub in Dublin, it is in a corner of McDaid's that he made himself at home with a glass and typewriter.

This somewhat squarish bar room with its cool, high ceilings has been a special port of call for writers, artists and would-be literati for the past 120 years. In the 40s and 50s, on a good evening you could easily have been entertained by the literary supernova of Behan, Patrick Kavanagh, and Brian O'Nolan, any one of whom would have been more than enough for you, and who were at times, too much for each other.

O'Nolan, a notorious tease, would let fly at Kavanagh with resultant exchanges that are still remembered and quoted. A case in point: "You're nothing but a minor poet," O'Nolan is reported to have once flung out, to which Kavanagh, after a sufficient pause, replied, "Since Homer, we all are."

These days the pub is bearing up well, refusing to be a prisoner of its own glittering past, yet holding on to its character and integrity. A bright new bar in the traditional idiom has been added to one side of the room and soft music rather than the garrulous ripostes of its most famous customers, have opened McDaid's to new possibilities and an atmosphere in which the young and the well-to-do rub shoulders with the "regulars."

MOTHER REDCAP'S

Christchurch Backlane 8

One of the new-style pubs (this one is four years old) that are big and barnlike spaces, refurbished in light pine and exposed brick. There are bright fires and various conversational enclosures are created by using raised platforms and wooden planks as dividers.

Mother Redcap's is a rugby and football pub and features the shirts of various team stars as well as pennants.

Check out the market behind the pub.

Traditional music (look in newspaper for current schedule).

JOHN MULLIGAN'S

8 Poolbeg Street

If you wish to be counted as a true connoisseur of Dublin's best pubs, this one is a must. Licensed in 1782, Mulligan's is one of the oldest pubs in the city and certainly one of the most characterful. The exterior sports some nice old lettering on the windows: WINE, WHISKEY-BONDER, SPIRITS, and over the door: PUBLIC BAR. The pint here has long been reputed to be one of the best in Dublin and has been enjoyed by many famous names, among them John F. Kennedy, who stopped in as a regular in 1945 during his days working for the Hearst newspaper chain.

As a matter of fact, Mulligan's has long been a favourite with journalists (the office of two of the national dailies are in the vicinity), who find its dark, simple recesses to their liking. You'll find students here too.

Mulligan's was associated with the Theatre Royal which was located across the street and its walls are decorated with old posters from those heady days. Here too, were held the meetings of that most congenial group, "The Society For the Preservation of The Dublin Accent." Today's regulars testify that it is alive and well. Thank God.

There are three bars and a large upstairs lounge with heavy Victorian furniture where the merchants from the local Corn Exchange used to banquet regularly.

A wide variety of Dubliners seem to have a very particular, almost reverential affection for this pub. It is always referred to as "Oh, yes, Mulligan's of Poolbeg Street," to distinguish it from lesser

Mulligan's. And then, invariably, the speaker will add, "now there's a really great pub." I agree.

Neary's

1 Chatham Street

While some pubs are hidden away (The Stag's Head or The Brazen Head, for example), you'll have no trouble at all locating Neary's. First because it's so well-known that you can ask anyone to direct you there; and second because it's easily recognisable. On either side of the Chatham Street entrance are two unusual beacons—large bronze arms that seem to spring out of the brick, their hands holding aloft lamps as though to guide the lost to a safe haven. And so it is too, when you enter and find yourself in a decorous Edwardian interior, elegant with well-preserved shining brass, milky glass gas lamps, and satiny mahogany. The feeling is rather like that of a good "club"—a sense of tradition upheld to just the pleasant side of stuffiness.

Upstairs is a calm, pleasantly-lit lounge, in contrast to the downstairs bar which seems like a Victorian stage set filled with a "mod" cast. With the Gaiety Theatre literally at the back door, chances are that many of the "cast" really *are* actors, or in any case, after-theatre revellers.

Neary's has a distinguished past as a host to a variety of figures in "arts and letters" and is still a favourite classy meeting place to start out an evening's adventure.

The smoked salmon here is a justly famous speciality of the house as are oysters. Also offered is a good selection of salads and sandwiches and the home-made wholemeal bread is definitely "to write home about."

O'Donoghue's

15 Merrion Row

This famous pub, just a few doors down from St Stephen's Green, is a mecca for traditional Irish music. It was the launching spot for *The Dubliners*, and is still a favourite venue for traditional bands both famous and "wanna-be."

At O'Donoghue's the music is impromptu and inspired, and there are often two sessions going on at once; one in the front room where the bar is and one in the back room, where the salmon-coloured walls are covered with photos of the musicians who have played there over the years.

The air is thick with smoke, smiles abound and people move from the bar through the crowd juggling four and five pints for their friends.

The music is listened to with a light reverence that is easy to fall into and the proceedings are aided by the atmosphere of an authentic old pub that has not been "updated."

Come early at weekends if you want a seat.

The Old Stand

37 Exchequer Street

The Old Stand is named after the old rugby stand on Landsdowne Road and it does attract a sporting crowd as well as students and business people. The décor is decidedly sporty and very cheerful; note the horseshoe bar with its Welsh dresser and the gleaming horse brasses.

The Old Stand's hot lunches, which are known all over town, can be enjoyed in cosy compartments along the walls, at the bar counter or in the back room.

This is an upbeat, chatty, crowded place perfect for dropping into for a meal or a drink before going on to a match or race meeting.

The Palace Bar

21 Fleet Street

This unspoiled pub is to be recommended for its delightful back room where the lovely Dublin light streams down through a milky skylight, adding a special glow to the paintings, the old leather chairs and the faces of the drinkers. Once *the* meeting place for writers, journalists and politicians (R.M. Smyllie, the salty editor of *The Irish Times*, used to hold forth in one corner, christened "the intensive care unit" by the pub's wags), The Palace is still a very popular talk-shop for writers, students and journalists (the office of *The Irish Times* is just around the corner). The walls of the back room are covered with photos and drawings of famous writers who've frequented it and partaken of a drop or two.

The Portobello

33 South Richmond Street
and 1 Charlemont Hall

The Portobello is well over a century old. The pub, now housed in a Victorian building, was formerly a Georgian house and was first opened in 1806.

The two downstairs bars are in the traditional Irish style, and the upstairs lounge, which opens at 7.30 p.m., has a lovely open fire. The large windows offer a fine view of the Grand Canal and approach roads, which was why the rebels of the Easter uprising used this pub as a command post. The scars of battle are still to be seen here — bullet-marks in some of the wooden beams downstairs.

RYAN'S

28 Parkgate Street

Ryan's is a favourite of mine. This however does not make me very original. *Everyone* loves Ryan's. Here we have a beautiful, tranquil jewel of a pub, lovingly and meticulously maintained since its opening in the Gay 90s. The marvellously carved bar takes up the centre of the room, rather like a sleek, mahogany ship lying at berth. The lighting is warmly dim; the ceiling is very high and crowned with a smoky, mirrored skylight, and the bar is presided over by Mr Ryan, the epitome of old world charm in his waistcoat and crisp white shirt.

In the front of the pub is a roomy snug which connects directly to the bar via a little window through which the barman passes the deservedly famous libations. Actually, the barman at Ryan's wields a special power; he controls the latch to the snug so that you can enter or leave only at his discretion. When you've finished with your tête-à-tête, you ring a little bell and he releases the lock on the door. So if you want to be captivated in more ways than one, Ryan's is your spot.

There is an equally beautiful back room and an upstairs restaurant which serves excellent food.

Ryan's also boasts one of the most elegant "rest-rooms" in town. Even the toilet is vintage polished mahogany.

SEARSON'S

42 Baggot Street Upper

This very large pub was renovated in 1991 to reflect the traditional turn-of-the-century style, and the job was a good one. There's a beautiful, free-standing, horseshoe bar in the centre of the front room, and the spacious back room, pleasantly conservatory-like with plants and a skylight, has been skilfully divided into intimate nooks and crannies. The carvery meats and pub food are tasty and varied, and on a sunny day you can have lunch outside on the brick patio.

Thursday nights are special: the pub offers traditional set dancing and new, young bands.

SINNOT'S

26 St Stephen's Green

At the top of pedestrianised Grafton Street, Dublin's teeming, vital main artery, is the Stephen's Green Centre, a glass domed shopping emporium-cum-mall. Here you'll find Sinnot's, unusual because although it has a store front at street level, it's actually underground. The five-year-old pub is owned by Liam O'Dwyer, one of the enterprising O'Dwyer brothers, who was told by less venturesome experts that his new pub "would never work." Satisfyingly enough for Liam, the pundits were wrong—it not only works very well, but is a good pub too.

Another innovative twist: this is a smoke-free pub, a boon for the increasing number of those who want to get away from the nicotine clouds endemic to regular pubs.

SLATTERY'S

129 Capel Street

The nineteenth century façades on this street are important fragments of bygone Dublin and beneath much of the street lie the remains of St Mary's Abbey and the early Cistercians who built it. P. & W. Slattery's, Grocers, Wine and Spirit Merchants, established in a mid-nineteenth-century structure for many years now, is one of the most important traditional music pubs in the city. Its influence has been seminal since the '60s, helped in no small measure by having two entertainment lounges, one upstairs, one downstairs. Songs, ballads, traditional, folk, jazz, blues, all can be heard here — check the evening papers first.

The ground floor bar was modernised in recent years as was the façade outside, and good efforts have been made to restore the fine elevation to its original Victorian splendour.

The Stag's Head

1 Dame Court

Part of the fun of going to the Stag's Head for the first time is finding it, hidden away as it is in the heart of the city centre. Walk up Dame street, Dublin's principal commercial and insurance street, keeping an alert eye out for a passageway indicated in the pavement by a mosaic image of a stag's head. Duck through to cobblestoned Dame Court, where you'll discover a red-brick Victorian building complete with bottleglass windows and scrolled doorway. It looks very much the tavern of old etchings, as well it might; it has remained unchanged since it began serving Dubliners in 1890.

Inside is a delightfully warm atmosphere, all old leather, polished wood and ornate brass. The original stained-glass windows shed a gentle light, each sporting a stag's head in the centre of a leafy scroll. The bar is very typical of Dublin. It is one of the long type, (mahogany capped with red Connemara marble) with its length neatly punctuated by exquisite partitions.

Above the bar, mildly surveying his domain, is the proud namesake of the place—a seven point stag's head. The Victorian smoking room at the end of the bar is lit with a skylight and is now used as a luncheon bar.

One of the main attractions of the place is the excellence of its food and drink, and its menu chalked up daily for the crowds of lunchtime habitués who flood in from the surrounding offices and nearby Dublin Stock Exchange. (A tip: if you're lunching here make sure to arrive a few minutes before noon or just before 2.00 p.m., or you're like to have a long wait).

Tuesday and Friday nights (call to see if this schedule has changed, 679 3701) go downstairs for an evening of traditional and not so traditional balladeering. You'll find that the crowd is refreshing, only a smattering of tourists among a large number of Irish young people who know most of the songs and who sing along in high good humour. The atmosphere is spirited (pun intended), with audience and entertainers exchanging jokes and friendly gibes. Everyone talks to everyone, and you might even be invited home to a further singsong.

TONER'S

139 Lower Baggot Street

One of that very special breed, Dublin pubs of real character, Toner's is a Victorian bar with a story you can easily read in its architecture and accoutrements. The story begins with Andrew Rogers, who had his first pub and grocery shop in Baggot Street in 1817 and later acquired and developed the present site and the newly opened side entrance to his wine stores. By 1842 "Andrew Rogers Grocer and Wine Merchant" was a favourite in the town.

Toner's is still proud to have been the only pub in Dublin ever visited by W.B. Yeats. Apparently, he was brought there by that great wit and bon vivant Oliver St John Gogarty and sat in the snug to the left of the door where he was brought a sherry. After downing the drink, he is supposed to have risen and said "I've seen a pub. Now would you kindly take me home," and without a glance at the colourful décor went out and stepped into a waiting carriage.

For anyone with a feeling for social history, Toner's is a delight to the senses, from the old storage drawers for teas and groceries to the pump handles of the old beer machines, the nicotined walls and ceilings and the reminders that not all drinks served here were alcoholic . . . Hovenden and Orrs, Aerated Lithia waters and hot bitters, which long ago were manufactured a stone's throw away on Steven's Green, are still recalled among the old advertisements which hang on the wall. Bring a friend during the day and meet some solid pint drinkers. Spend some time in the "Yeats' snug," and drink a sherry in the poet's honour, even if he didn't understand pubs.

The Waterloo House/Ryan's

36 Baggot Street Upper

What's lovely about the Waterloo, is that it's meant for conversation. Established 1899, it is a lovely evocation of the Victorian era at its least fussy. There are two entrances: one to the smaller back lounge bar, and one into the main pub. I took a little spiked tea in the back room on a blustery day. It was the ideal place to be. The room is long and narrow, with a small, intimate bar and comfortable seating at a few tables. Rain was drumming down on the skylight, a man at the bar was reading a novel over a cup of coffee and the rest of the clientele were paying silent homage to a broadcast of the race track results. Etched glass windows separate the lounge from the main bar and the bartenders pop them open to talk back and forth.

The main room has an exceptionally nice plasterwork ceiling and you can rest your elbows on the original mahogany bar, which according to the owner is worth close to £100,000. The ceiling is high, and there's a lovely sense of spacious hush and peace here.

The Waterloo, so named because it faces Waterloo Road, has been owned and run by John Ryan for thirty two years, and presently, his son Andrew is assisting him.

"Paddy Kavanagh used to come in here," Andrew tells me, "he wasn't too bad, but Behan was barred for looking for a fight—he'd challenge anybody. My father had a pub in the Liberties (a very tough part of Dublin) for eight years before he opened this one, so he was fairly well used to this type of customer."

The Temple Bar District: Dublin's "Happening" Centre

A brief history and pub guide

Temple Bar is an area of Dublin that is bounded by Dame and Lord Edward Streets, Westmoreland Street and the parallel quays along the River Liffey. People attempting to describe the flavour and character of this central network of cobbled streets sometimes borrow words that actually apply to other cities. Designations like the Left Bank, Greenwich Village, the Latin Quarter and Soho, are bandied about. While such comparisons do capture the artsy atmosphere and Bohemian attitude of the area, none of these imported labels really fits—because Temple Bar is uniquely, heart and soul, a Dublin phenomenon.

In lanes that were laid out in the eighteenth century, in buildings that are 200 years old, artists, designers and young entrepreneurs have set up small exciting galleries, fun shops, art studios and a scintillating variety of good to excellent restaurants.

The people that hang out in this district are mostly young, but let's not be ageist about this! Anyone who is looking for a relaxed, easy-going place that has lots to offer should take a look. It's the place to go for "alternative" shopping, for ethnic food and certainly for fun in the many theatres, cinemas, nightclubs and bars.

As you thread your way through the cheerful crowds, it's hard to imagine that the area had its beginnings as a monastic retreat for an order of Augustinian Hermits in 1259. As Dublin grew, the hermits fled to more appropriate wilds, and eventually, in the seventeenth century, the land was deeded to loyal servants of the British crown, most particularly to one William Temple who built a house and gardens here. In those times, a "bar" was the name of a walkway by a river, so the path used by the Temple family became known as the Temple Bar.

By the eighteenth century the area had become an extravagant mixture of brothels, craftsmen, artisans, shipping companies and merchants all existing cheek by jowl in the jumble of crowded lanes and alleys, and in the following century it expanded into a lively centre for the clothing trade.

Nineteenth and twentieth century industrialisation, mass production, and importation killed the trades of the area, and by 1970 it was in a severe enough decline for the Dublin Transport Authority to conceive a plan for razing the buildings and creating a bus depot and transport centre that would have covered seven acres (2.8 ha).

Realising that it would take a long time for them to set this plan in motion, the Transport Board decided to rent out, on very short term leases, some of the small shops and buildings. Enter a life-giving influx of the young, the "hip," and the talented, looking for cheap space for their studios, shops and restaurants, and so the rebirth of Temple Bar began.

In 1985, a coalition of conservationists, local residents and traders lobbied to preserve the area under government protection. They won their cause, with the result that Temple Bar, now safely designated an historic area, is rapidly becoming the cultural hub of Dublin. Everywhere you look buildings are being restored and streets pedestrianised. The new Irish Film Centre has been established here in a resurrected Quaker Meeting House, and buildings are being restored to house a Music Centre and a Children's Meeting House. New buildings for a Multi Media Centre and a Centre for Photography are under construction.

For me, the spirit of Temple Bar appeared one noon-time in the person of a one-man band set up in one of the alleyways. Here was a young man in jeans and scarf, an umbrella fixed over his head, operating what the sign in front of him said was "The Elastic Band." While he expertly delivered a truly haunting rendition of a country blues song, playing guitar and harmonica as well as singing, his tapping foot set into motion his accompanists on drums and tambourine; several charming, "Sesame Street" style stuffed animals and a tin woman and man. The tin folk were ingenious characters, with children's sneakers for feet, rubber gloves for hands, and hip dark glasses covering their eyes. The tin woman had a kerchief, the man a cap.

The thing that mesmerised the crowd, myself included, was not only the charming originality of "the band," but the fact that the music was *really good.*

Temple Bar Pubs

The pubs within the Temple Bar boundary are a diverse lot. On the one hand there are places like the Norseman, Flannery's, The Crane and Rumpoles which attract the young, bohemian, artsy (often loud) crowd that the area is famous for, while on the other there are quieter and more sedate spots like The City Hall Inn or The Oak which appeal to a slightly older crowd.

There are so many pubs in the area, so different from each other and so close together that Temple Bar might just be the most perfect venue for a good old-fashioned and rewarding pub crawl (no need to worry about the breathalyser here).

Opening hours Monday-Saturday: 10.30 a.m.—11 p.m. (11.30 in summer).

THE AULD DUBLINER

17 Anglesea Street

It's easy to spot this pub; there's a wonderful mural painted on the side of the building showing an old Dublin dock character (a nod to the area's past) with a big beer belly, a captain's hat and a newspaper sticking out of his pocket. He's looking askance at a dog who is lifting his leg against the building. Behind this character is painted a stained-glass window bearing the words "The Auld Dubliner."

Inside, the pub is quiet and cosy, with exposed brick walls and the original floor. At the bar, you'll find a good mix of regulars and Temple Bar habitués. "Me Ma and Pa used to drink here thirty years ago, after shopping," one customer told me.

Traditional music on Sunday mornings and Tuesday nights. Coddle, a traditional Dublin dish of boiled streaky bacon, sausages and potatoes is served at lunchtimes from Monday-Friday.

CITY HALL INN

75 Dame Street

Once reputed to have been owned by the singer Joseph Locke, this pub has a comfortable, suburban feel that attracts a more "settled" clientele.

THE CRANE BAR

34 Essex Street

The sign, painted in austere gold lettering on the front reads, "quite Possibly importers of Fine Wine Since 1830," a fair indication that this is a pub that doesn't take itself too seriously. Extremely popular with true Temple Bar fans, it's sparsely furnished and quite large, though the crowd still tends to spill out into the street on fine summer evenings. Take care not to do yourself injury on the huge piece of sculpture just inside the door.

DANIEL O'CONNELL BAR

22 Aston Quay

This popular pub tends more towards a comfortable, lounge bar, city centre mood than a Temple Bar atmosphere, but there's good conversation to be had here.

Flannery's/The Temple Bar

44 Temple Bar

The owners have pulled out the depressing, formica and plastic tat of the '70s and restored this pub to its former stained wood glory. Splendid open fires blazing in the winter. Packed out at night with a lively, young, arty crowd.

Foggy Dew

1 Fownes Street Upper

A tiny bar, so small you almost *have* to talk to the person next to you. A favourite hangout for musicians.

Ha'penny Bridge

42 Wellington Quay

The Ha'penny Bridge, a beautifully crafted, metal pedestrian bridge across the Liffey, is a famous Dublin landmark. It was erected in 1816 so that Dubliners could go to the music hall in Crow Street without the bother of a murky ferry crossing, and all for the toll of a mere ha'penny.

The bridge, much photographed, is still there, a few doors down the quay from the pub that bears its name. The place is a busy, friendly traditional pub much frequented by those who have always worked in the area.

Irish Film Centre Bar

6 Eustace Street

An ultra modern bar in this building that has been totally renovated. Fun for film buffs.

Norseman Pub

Essex Street East

The original Temple Bar hangout, an amicable, authentic pub dominated by a traditional mahogany bar, and still the home base for those who pioneered the district. Attracts an appealing mix of locals, artists and theatre-goers that tends to spill out into the street on a fine night, joining up with the crowd from nearby Flannery's. Especially popular on weekends when the convivial atmosphere is conducive to amusing encounters with strangers.

Music plays a big role at the Norseman where you'll find good traditional sessions.

THE OAK

81 Dame Street

A small, intimate pub, perfect for a quiet rendezvous or pre-theatre drink.

THE OLIVER ST JOHN GOGARTY

57 Fleet Street

Named after the famous Dublin wit, surgeon, writer and pal of James Joyce, this pub gives a pleasant feel of light and air. The downstairs room has an island bar, stone floors, old butcher blocks and machine parts as tables, kegs as stools and several secluded areas offering a sense of privacy.

Upstairs, the function room and restaurant are tastefully uncluttered, with wide board floors, wooden beams and attractive pine furniture. The food is good and Gogarty's is a favourite with Dubliners of all generations and professions. The pub is often chosen as a venue for literary events, so watch the papers to see what's happening here.

Traditional music on Saturdays (no cover charge).

RUMPOLES

18 Parliament Street

First colonised by actors looking for a quiet, emptyish place for an after-show drink. Actors and low-key theatre folk still make up the loyal core of aficionados, but Rumpoles has grown to be one of the most popular bars in the area. Live music on Wednesday and Thursday nights.

Hotel Pubs

YESTERDAY'S BAR

Bloom's Hotel, Anglesea Street

This pub is found in Bloom's Hotel (named after Joyce's hero, of course), a first-class establishment in the heart of the Temple Bar district. Yesterday's belies its name—it is quite trendy and "today," popular especially with the office workers of the area and very busy at weekends.

ALFIE BYRNE'S

The Conrad Hotel

As you enter the pub from the lobby of the five star Hotel Conrad, notice the decorative tile on the wall showing a jaunty fellow holding an umbrella and tipping his hat to you. This is Alfie Byrne (1882–1956 as the tile says), one of Dublin's most beloved Lord Mayors, who endeared himself to the city's street urchins by always carrying some sweets. He's shown here standing in front of the Lord Mayor's Mansion, and I'm sure he'd be quite pleased with the pub that bears his name.

Alfie Byrne's is an attractive place, with a long, sunken gallery looking out onto a courtyard and fountain. The fountain itself, a lyrical statue of a swirl of ducks, beautifully utilises stones that come from the streams and rivers of the West of Ireland. On mild days at noon, flocks of office workers take lunch out here, lifting grateful faces to the sun.

The pub's floors are marble and the décor exudes an overall sense of polished brass and dark oak. Illustrations of traditional Irish pubs enliven the walls.

Piano and music at weekends (jazz on Saturday). The varied menu is excellent, which means the place is packed at lunch, as is the case too for Friday nights. Sunday night is the night for Alfie Byrne's if you're looking for peace and quiet.

The Garage Bar
The Clarence Bar
The Clarence Hotel
Wellington Quay
A youngish crowd is permanently parked in the Garage Bar with its eclectic mix of Bus Eireann seating, fake fur stools, spit-and-sawdust floor and conversationally challenging music.

In utter contrast, the Clarence Bar attracts refugees from the madlands of packed city pubs, seeking comfy leather armchairs, low decibel chat and a calming country hotel atmosphere.

The Shelbourne Hotel Bar
The Horseshoe Bar
The Shelbourne Hotel
The Shelbourne is the quintessential, Grande Dame of Dublin's hotels, with its Victorian elegance and British style drawing room, lobby and lounge. The Shelbourne Bar picks up on this mood. It's a "clubby" place with a high-gloss floor and marble fireplaces. When empty it looks like a turn-of-the-century ball-room waiting for couples to tango. Along one wall is a huge,

burnished bar, featuring copies of the famous neo-classical Egyptian statues that have stood guard outside the hotel for a century. Do not come here on a Thursday or Friday night unless you really love a crowd scene. Extremely popular with the "in" professional crowd and legal eagles, *the* place to rub elbows with a Guinness heiress.

The Shelbourne's Horseshoe Bar across the lobby is less densely populated and has a pleasantly masculine, leather and tobacco atmosphere. There are plenty of upholstered nooks to sit in.

Late Night Pubs

BAD BOB'S BACKSTAGE BAR

34 East Essex Street

Dublin's best known, late night music place, as the weekend queue out the door testifies. A lively, fun spot with country and Cajun music seven nights a week. Three floors, live bands downstairs, a bar in the middle and a lively, late night disco on the top. Upstairs bar open from 5.30 p.m., other levels 10.30 p.m.–2.00 a.m. Full licence. Admission charge. Over 23's.

THE ROCK GARDEN

3A Crown Alley

The interior is all sheet metal chic and bare brick. At present, Dublin's newest rock venue, the Rock Garden averages three bands a night ranging from established Irish artists and visiting international acts to new bands. "Breakthrough" night on Monday and Tuesday gives hopefuls a chance to try out. The full late night bar until 2.00 p.m. is a rocking good attraction. Live music 8.00 p.m.–2.20 a.m. nightly. Free lunchtime gig on Saturday afternoons. Upstairs, there's a casual, fun restaurant and diners get in to gig for half price. Otherwise, admission charges vary. Over 18's.

Morning After Pubs, or "Early Houses"

Some people like to wrap up a night of joyful carousing with a final, last stop in an "early house." Go to Smithfield for a taste of dawn at market pubs full of country people, fruit sellers and farmers. In Stoneybatter there's Delaney's and Keogh's, and for a touch of dockside Dublin, there's Valance Murphy's.

Dublin's Suburban Pubs
See entries for Booterstown, Dalkey, Dun Laoghaire, Howth and Glencullen.

DUN LAOGHAIRE, CO. DUBLIN

THE PURTY KITCHEN

A smartly attractive and large pub with an exceptionally good, full bar menu. Specialities: seafood, prawns, trout, and seafood chowder.

GLASSON, NR ATHLONE, CO. WESTMEATH

GROGAN'S

A real find of a pub in a pretty village. Family-run and old-fashioned, with a low-ceilinged cosy room in the front, an open fire in the back, and a beer garden outside. Simon Grogan is the man in the kitchen here, and he knows how to set out a delicious plate of salads and snacks.

GLENCULLEN, CO. DUBLIN

FOX'S

Here's a way to have the best of country and city at the same time—a pub that is stunningly situated in the rugged Dublin Mountains yet only 40 minutes from the city centre.

Fox's (est. 1798) is understandably hugely popular with the city folk. The pub is frequented by a wonderfully varied bunch which a friend describes as "everything from solicitors to posers, from artists to petrol attendants. They flock there on bicycles, in leather upholstered Porsches and in four-wheel-drive vehicles with furry dice dangling from the rearview mirror."

As if the sweet country air and the delightful views aren't enough, Fox's offers some of the best food, mood and music around.

The seafood is fresh as an ocean breeze, and there's a great choice: Irish wild smoked salmon, crab, prawns, mussels, oysters, lobster . . . you name it, they have it. My own personal favourite is mussels in a broth so tasty that it makes you want to get up and sing.

And there's no problem if that's what you want to do. This pub has excellent traditional entertainment, ballads, bands and/or dancing seven nights a week in three different rooms. The craic is so good that the place seems to just lift off the mountain with the sheer joyful energy of it all.

Fox's is large and rambling and care has been taken to preserve the traditional aura of turf fires, stone floors and antique bric-a-brac without getting too "twee."

Howth, Co. Dublin

The Abbey Tavern

Howth is a beauty spot, yachting centre and fashionable suburb by the sea nine miles (14.5 km) from the centre of Dublin. For the ultimate in romantic walks, take a stroll on the meandering pathways of the Hill of Howth. The wild, heathery view, the cries of gulls and the sweetly scented wind will make it clear to you why James Joyce chose this spot for the final and poetically erotic scene of his book, *Ulysses*. Go to the Hill at twilight, drench yourself in beauty and then adjourn for an evening of revelry at the Abbey.

The Abbey is something of a Dublin institution and although it is a mecca for tourists, local people appreciate it as well. There's been a tavern here since 1740 (part of the tavern itself dates back to the fifteenth century), and the Abbey per se has been operating unchanged for the last forty years. Built against the wall of a centuries-old abbey (hence the name), it's a traditional pub with turf fires, original stone walls, a lot of timber, good pints, honest drink, ballads in the back room and a surprisingly good restaurant upstairs.

Kells, Co. Meath

Yes, this ancient town in the wooded part of the River Blackwater valley *is* the birthplace of one of the world's great treasures, the ninth-century illuminated manuscript of the Four Gospels that is called the Book of Kells. Although the original Book itself is kept at the Trinity College Library in Dublin, you can marvel at a facsimile here in Kells, at St Columba's Church.

O'Shaughnessy's
Just behind St Columba's Church is O'Shaughnessy's, a new pub pleasantly decorated in the old-time style. The pub is a perfect place to stop in for a pint and a bite. The food is both good and reasonably-priced, a winning combination. The menu is nicely varied: Irish stew, chicken or beef curry, lasagne, quiche and pizza.

Kilcullen, Co. Kildare

Two miles (3 km) south of this little town, at Old Kilcullen, are the remains of a round tower and three ninth-century high crosses.

The Hideout
This pub is a large complex of rooms with dark walls, fireplaces, historical artifacts, stuffed animals and fish gracing the walls and corners.

But the prized artifact here is one that might be considered in questionable, if not ghoulish taste by some. I would not have believed it if I had not seen it with "me very own eyes." Here, on display in a glass case, is the actual, entire, mummified arm of the great Irish boxer Dan Donnelly. Go ahead—call me a liar—but look for yourself.

I was not informed as to how The Hideout came into possession of this portion of poor Dan's anatomy, but it does make for interesting speculation. Dan was a celebrated boxer, a giant among men. A few miles away, at Donnelly's Hollow at the eastern end of The Curragh, Donnelly fought a famous match in 1815 in which he defeated the English champion George Cooper. You can still see the outsize prints his feet made that day as he left the Hollow. They have been retrodden into permanence by countless visitors since, perhaps in the hope of receiving osmotically some of the giant's prodigious strength.

Kilkenny, Co. Kilkenny

Kilkenny is not only a beautiful medieval town with a modern, cosmopolitan heartbeat, it's the national centre for crafts and design. The shops and galleries here are filled with an impressive

and tantalising array of original works and giftware in glass, clay, precious metals, leather and textiles. Twenty minutes away, the little town of Bennetsbridge has become a centre for the studios and workshops of such famous artisans as potter Nicholas Mosse and Mary O'Gorman. They are open to the public and it's not only fun to see creativity in action, but you can also come away with some real bargains in "seconds" ware.

EAMON LANGTON'S

69 John's Street

When you're in Sydney you have to see the Opera House, in New York the Empire State building is a must, and in Kilkenny no visit is complete without paying a call to Eamon Langton's.

Over the years, this justly famous pub has won so many Best Food and Best Pub awards that Eamon Langton was recently asked to stand down and give someone else a chance.

The minute you enter the front room you know that you are in good hands. Naturally, there's a lovely fireplace with a fine, carved wooden mantelpiece. The ceiling is low and the atmosphere is a warm one, of dark wood, burgundy leather, and tasteful but not oppressive affluence.

The "back room" is not a term that should be used to describe the restaurant that occupies the rear of the building. No indeed, for here we have a design triumph. The overall impression is that of skylights, green plants and a sense of graceful atrium airiness — the walls virtually stream light from tiers of tall Gothic-style windows that rise two storeys high. The view is of a series of pretty gardens and patios which are open for the sun-lover on fine days.

Dancing on Tuesday and Saturday evenings. Bar food and restaurant meals.

KYTELER'S INN

This inn has proffered victuals and spirits for six hundred years. These days, the ground floor is a restaurant and bar, cleanly and beautifully renovated in pine. Downstairs however, the thirteenth century lives. A deep-set window overlooks St Cieran's well, which outdates even the inn itself. The original stone pillars reach floor to ceiling in this shadowy, candlelit cellar, which hasn't changed much from the fourteenth century, when Dame Alice Kyteler made the tavern a place of merrymaking.

Apparently, Dame Alice was good at more than merrymaking—she was a banker and moneylender and laid four husbands to rest in the Kilkenny graveyard—under what were supposedly suspicious circumstances. In 1324 she was tried for witchcraft and condemned to be burned at the stake. She and her disciples were accused of sacrificing black cocks to the Devil and brewing foul mixtures of their entrails, then mixing them with herbs, insects, the hair and nails of unbaptized children, and dead men (the husbands?).

Alice escaped to England, but her maid, Petronilla, was not as lucky and was burned.

There's a life-size doll of Dame Alice presiding over the goings on in the cellar, and at Hallowe'en, the pub puts on a joyous celebration in her macabre honour.

TYNAN'S BRIDGE HOUSE

St. John's Bridge

This is a pub you'll want to take home with you. Tynan's, just beside the Nore, was consistently recommended to me as one of Ireland's best. With its beautifully preserved appointments, it is an antiquarian's delight.

Tynan's was a pharmacy and grocery store, and Michael Tynan has owned and operated the pub since 1919. It is considered by many to be the most genuine and interesting pub in Kilkenny.

In perfect rows of shiny wood behind the front bar are ranks of drawers marked CLOVES, CITRON, ALMONDS, RICE, SAGO. An iron rail remembers when it used to support flitches of bacon from its hooks, an intricate old clock chimes the hour, a two-hundred-year-old scale, with its wonderful little cup weights, stands on the bar; and all is lit nostalgically by old, globed gas lamps

in perfect working order. All this and more . . . as the ads used to say.

I sat down at the central bar, a kind of large island that takes up most of the room, and ordered a Smithwick's ale. An elderly gentleman with a kindly, ruddy face was seated next to me. "Damned good choice," he commented. "The name's Walter B. Smithwick," he said, holding out his hand and enjoying my flabbergasted expression.

Smithwick's, now part of The Guinness Group, have been brewing in Kilkenny since 1710. The brewery is built on the site of a twelfth-century Franciscan monastery, whose Romanesque tower is now surrounded by loading docks, beer kegs and trucks — quite an expansion of the bit of brewing done by the good brothers, its former occupants.

Mr Smithwick kindly invited me to visit him for breakfast at Kilkreen Lodge, the Smithwick homestead for several centuries. I was pleased to hear that I was partaking of rashers and eggs under the same roof that had sheltered such distinguished visitors as William Congreve and Jonathan Swift. After coffee in the greenhouse, Mr Smithwick took me for a tour of Kilkenny. I guess I just picked the right ale that day.

LEIGHLINBRIDGE, CO. CARLOW

THE LORD BAGENAL INN

While this tavern, just off the M9 Waterford-Carlow road, is a great halfway house, it's really more than that. The Lord Bagenal has gained an impressive reputation nationwide for its exceptional food and service. Here you can get anything from a snack to go with your pint to a full meal. The choices include home-made pâtés, local steaks, seafood from the Wexford coast, wild Slaney salmon and good farmhouse cheeses. An unusual touch: an excellent wine list at reasonable prices.

If you're travelling with children, the Lord Bagenal is the perfect cure for the "restless-in-the-car blues." There's a playground just outside the tavern, and a picnic area down beside the nearby river.

Lissoy, Co. Westmeath

Bordering Lough Ree, nine miles (14.5 km) north of Athlone, is Oliver Goldsmith country. The eighteenth-century poet and writer, author of *She Stoops To Conquer*, was raised in the little town of Lissoy or Auburn, made famous in his poem, *The Deserted Village*.

Three Jolly Pigeons

A true eighteenth-century alehouse, with the appropriate accoutrements and good chat, not necessarily about Goldsmith.

Maynooth, Co. Kildare

Noel Cassidy's

50 College Green

This pub was suggested to me by the poet Derek Mahon. "It's a crazy kind of place," he told me, "with a huge Gothic room full of Grecian pillars and art deco stuff."

He's right, the place is wildly amusing, especially since it's in a university town where classicism can be a serious business.

Monasterboice, Co. Louth

In this secluded spot six miles (9.5 km) northwest of Drogheda, St Biuthe established a monastery circa the fifth century, the nucleus of what was to become an important centre of learning. The ruins

are impressive and include a round tower with a door six feet (1.8 m) above ground level. Monasterboice is also the site of one of Ireland's finest high crosses — seventeen feet (5 m) tall — the surface of which writhes with sculpted figures and designs.

The Monasterboice Inn

Between Drogheda and Dundalk

A modern pub, busy and full of local people enthusiastically enjoying themselves. Very popular with people driving up and down the Belfast-Dublin corridor.

Moydow, Co. Longford

The Vintage

This is a pleasant bar with a side business of catering local functions and serving dinner three nights a week (plus lunch on Sundays). Or yet again maybe it's a restaurant and catering business that moonlights as a bar. Whatever the case, there's an open fire awaiting and you're sure to have a nice time .

Officially, they "don't do bar food," but if you ask nicely, their Irish "hospitality genes" just can't resist you, and they'll generally find something delicious to sneak you from the kitchen.

MULTIFARNUM, CO. WESTMEATH

A pretty, well-endowed village in the old sense, a calm place of the soil. Two lovely stone churches and a priest who preaches radical sermons.

SEAN MURTAGH'S

Renovated, but with nice timber floors. Westmeath people are not as outgoing as people from Clare or Kerry for instance, but if you just sit silent with them and wait a while, you'll soon feel a sense of comfortable companionship.

WEIR'S

A small, old-fashioned place, the genuine article. Spend an hour or so here and you'll depart in a tranquil mood.

MOONE, CO. KILDARE

A television quizmaster asked a Kildare contestant if he knew the author of *Gone With The Wind*. "No, but I know who trained him," came the response.

This is the county where the horse is king, the seat of the National stud at Tully and the home of the Curragh, the race course that is situated on a vast, dramatic plain where horses have been raced for the last two thousand years.

THE MOONE HIGH CROSS INN

If you're travelling in this part of the country, definitely plan your break here. Go for the genuine hospitality and excellent home cooking; pub lunch—bacon, cabbage and potatoes—a granny's type of lunch. Actually, there *is* a granny here, the convivial and spry Mrs Bridget Clynch (now past 80), head of the clan who run this rambling eighteenth century pub. Enjoy your meal and pints in the back bar by the open fire, and if you're very good, maybe Mrs Clynch will adopt you.

NAAS, CO. KILDARE

Naas, as a friend of mine says, is "a good town for pubs." The following is a selection offering you a choice of several styles. All the pubs line the main street.

The Hayden Pub

The crowd here is young and the pub lively. There's a lighted tank embedded in one wall, with interesting fish looking out at you. The pub is a good size and has an overall tone of rustic pine. Traditional music.

McCormack's

This pub has a little surprise for you. The front room is a plain, unvarnished, old-time kind of a place, where elderly men dream over their pints in the daytime. But go through the door to the back lounge and it's a different story. Here, under a skylight, a profusion of plants reach out prettily for the light. Interesting paintings and photographs hang on exposed brick walls and the impression is one of spareness on the right side of comfort.

I was introduced to this pub when I gave a lift to an old man in a cap who was hitch-hiking beside the road. As he got into my car, I warned the old gent that I wasn't used to Irish road rules yet, that in the United States, where I was from, we drive on the opposite side of the road and we don't have roundabouts. "Ah, don't worry yourself, girl," he said airily, "I've seen it all. Sure, I was a lorry driver for over thirty years."

However, after we went through several hilarious but hair-raising encounters with roundabouts, he fell quite silent, and by the time we reached Naas, I'd say he was more than ready to go to his local, which happened to be McCormack's.

Thomas Fletcher Commercial House and Wine Merchants

This pub is so clean and shiny it actually smells agreeably of polish. It's an old-fashioned place of true quality, with the muted, easy feel of days when there was time aplenty for just living. After negotiating the wildly busy main street outside, with its beeping bumper-to-bumper traffic, the sudden peace inside is a pleasant shock.

The room is like a long, narrow hall, and has a long, narrow mahogany bar to match, with a full complement of built-in spice drawers and shelves behind it. Traditional mahogany dividers with stained-glass panels section off the room, and in the front the huge and magnificent tea kegs are a reminder of when tea was packed and sold here.

Actually, you are not limited to drinking pints here. Even though you might like to see the barman pull the old brass pump handles, he'll be just as happy to serve you a nice cuppa for a few pence and for old time's sake.

NAVAN, CO. MEATH

BIRMINGHAM'S

Ludlow Street

An authentic, traditional pub which has remained unspoilt by time since its establishment in 1884. The beauty and craftsmanship of its old shop front, decorated at the top with a bank of colourful flowers, is impressively matched by the lovely carved wood of its interior. Impromptu "trad." and folk music.

NEWTON, CO. CARLOW

Tiny Carlow is shaped like an upside-down triangle. Small as it is, it's good climbing country, offering a pleasant upland in the north-west part of the county.

MICHAEL SMITH'S

Six miles (9.5 km) south of Athy is this unusual pub run by Michael Smith, the fourth generation to serve here as publican. The amusing centrepiece here is the grand piano, bought by Mr Smith in Germany many years ago and that is now valued at over £ 30,000. If you're lucky, someone will be tinkling the ivories when you come in.

PORTLAOISE, CO. LAOIS

EGAN'S

This pub on the Dublin-Cork road is a good pit-stop for a bit of grub after you've been dealing with the charioteers on the dual carriageway.

PROSPEROUS, CO. KILDARE

THE COTTAGE/GEORGE'S

Make sure you go to the back room of this pub, because that's what makes the place special. More than likely, this room was once the original main kitchen of a cottage that has seen a number of additions. There's a splendid, large fireplace with warm inglenooks, and in the place of honour above the mantel hangs a brass and leather plough horse harness. The little chamber is snugly outfitted with wainscotting and looks really cosy with tables and chairs of pine, old-fashioned bric-a-brac, kettles and pots, and a kitchen cupboard filled with crockery and glasses.

This is a back room of seductive intimacy, so if you have secrets you don't wish to share, don't come in and sit down here.

RATHNEW, CO. WICKLOW

HUNTER'S INN

A charming, old-fashioned inn with summer seating in an enchanting garden. A perfect stop for Irish Coffee or hot whiskey after a day in the mountains.

ROBERTSTOWN, CO. KILDARE

Crossing the River Liffey by an impressive aqueduct, you reach Robertstown, a canal-side village on the summit level of the Grand Canal, before it begins the descent to the Shannon Basin.

Conscious of the contribution the canal has made to their past, the townspeople have refurbished the old Canal Hotel as a museum, and you can enjoy an eighteenth-century candlelight banquet here during the summer months.

Robertstown has another claim to fame; it is the Falconry of Ireland, where a wide variety of hunting birds can be seen in action.

THE BARGE INN

Twilight is the ideal time to be in Robertstown if you can arrange it. Get a pint from the barman at the Barge Inn and sit on the canal wall. Soon you'll feel as though you've entered a time warp and landed in the eighteenth-century. The tranquillity is complete: swallows dart overhead and across the canal hayricks sport their white protective kerchiefs. The air over the water is still and smells faintly of turf smoke; the only sounds are those of dogs, birds and voices from inside the pub.

The Barge Inn is a regular kind of place—buy a round and you might hear tales of the heydays of canal boating.

Roundwood, Co. Wicklow

The Roundwood Inn

A truly authentic seventeenth-century inn nestled in unspoilt mountain beauty. The Roundwood combines the best qualities of a pub and a restaurant. The bar food is outstanding. Almost everything is locally grown or home-baked. There's Wicklow smoked trout, seafood from Greystones, venison, fresh vegetables, brown bread, and lamb stew. The triple liqueur parfait dessert is enough to make you come back the next day for a repeat performance.

In warm weather there's a secluded garden to sit in, and for those days when you need a fire, you can enjoy your food and/or drink in front of a huge log blaze.

Shannonbridge, Co. Offaly

The little village of Shannonbridge is so called after a graceful bridge of sixteen arches that spans the Shannon here. Four miles (6 km) north is Clonmacnoise, one of the most important historical sites in Ireland. St Ciaran founded a monastery here in 584 (the ruins are spectacular) which grew to become one of the most famous monastic cities of its time.

Michael Killeen's

Here's another one of those pubs that outgrew its origins as a pub-cum-grocer's without losing its charm. There are turf fires, beautiful pints and irreproachable Irish Coffees.

Wexford, Co. Wexford

From the dim times of antiquity the town of Wexford has looked out beyond the seas. Its origins are mysterious, but stone axes and artifacts reveal that organised communities thrived here around 2000 B.C., and over the years, the town on the Slaney River has become an international marketplace, bazaar and busy port.

Today's narrow winding streets, successors of ninth-century market trails, are lined with eighteenth-century houses and shop-fronts. The modern affliction of traffic jams seems oddly out of place.

Wexford is the home of an established event of international significance—the Wexford Opera Festival. The policy of the festival organisers is to produce rarely performed works with the best musicians, singers, conductors and producers available. In October, critics, talent scouts, socialites and opera lovers from all over make their way to Wexford.

The Raisin

Paul's Quay

You'll feel immediately welcome in this neat, small pub with a local feel. Truly a pub of character, where everything is genuinely traditional, including the lovely sign and red paint job.

Broade's

South Main Street

A friendly pub, traditional without being uncomfortable, where things have fortunately stayed the same for years. This is a "singing" pub, which is to say that the clientele often burst into song either singly or en masse. Let me hasten to add that it is not a commercial style singing pub, but one where songs just seem to happen, like spontaneous combustion.

Quite a few musicians come here, with the result that all types of songs are sung, from classical to folk and Irish traditional. If you're not too shy, you might treat everyone to a rendition of your own favourite ditty.

Wicklow, Co. Wicklow

> There's a primal quality to this country, the landscape has a wildness. The light is almost magical, though it does change a lot . . . It is said that you can have all four seasons in one day and I've known it to happen more than once in these past couple of months.
>
> *John Boorman, film director*
> *on shooting* Excalibur *at*
> *The National Film Studios in Wicklow*

Wicklow Arms/Delgany Inn

Here, in an old world seaside town that has the delights of the mountains nearby, is an inn that serves luscious meals in a comfortable, modern setting.

MUNSTER

ADARE, CO. LIMERICK

In 1976 Adare won first place in Ireland's National Tidy Towns competition. And no wonder. Driving into this town of 500 or so people is like entering one of those perfect little medieval towns pictured in children's books. Adare—even the name is lovely—means Fords of Oaks.

Along the banks of the River Maigue, in a rich and quiet setting, are thatched cottages, timbered black-and-white houses, and many romantic ruins and lichen-covered churches. There is a nine-hole golf course and fishing in the river—salmon, trout, and coarse fish. Coarse fishing is free; for salmon and trout, a licence is available from July to September.

You can follow the hounds from October to March, and the woods are full of game if you like less formal hunting—grouse, pheasant, snipe, woodcock, and duck. For information, inquire at the local sporting-goods store.

The village dates from the Norman conquest, but it owes its wide, shady main street and charming appearance to the third Earl of Dunraven, who designed and laid it out in the nineteenth century. His house and grounds are now the venue of a posh hotel, Adare Manor.

The eighteenth-century poet Sean O'Tuoma kept hens at Adare Manor for the lady of the manor. This was after he had run the pub he owned into bankruptcy. A generous and gregarious man, he advertised free tankards of ale to any fellow poet; there turned out to be quite a number of thirsty poets in the area. He was literally quaffed out of his pub, but not before he and his literary cronies had invented the art of the limerick. In honour of this gift to the world, every May there is a festival in the towns in the Maigue district, commemorating Sean and his pub.

ADARE MANOR BAR

The Tack Room

Downstairs in the cellar is a bar that is understatedly plush and fresh, done in clean white tones and wood. The Tack Room is now receiving a bit of local trade, which makes for a nice mix with the international and tourist crowd who are drawn here. Some say the best Irish coffee in Ireland is served right here in the Tack Room.

It has been said that one Irish coffee is enough, two is too many, and three not half enough. Unlike whiskey, which was discovered by the Irish well before A.D. 1178, Irish coffee is a recent invention. Its tasty advent is credited to Joe Sheridan, one-time chef at Shannon Airport.

Here follow instructions on the ceremony and preparation of this modern Irish contribution to the world's pleasures:

> ***The Official Formula***
> Warm a stemmed glass. Put into it a generous jigger of Bushmills whiskey, sugar to taste, and hot, strong, black coffee. Pour pure, fresh cream very slightly whipped (never commit the sin of using the aerated-can stuff) onto the top. To make sure that the cream floats gently on the surface of the coffee, it is a good idea to place a turned-over spoon at the edge of the glass just above the coffee line. Then pour the cream gently over the spoon until it rests lightly on top of the coffee mixture.
>
> Sip the result and join the connoisseurs who revel in the contrasting textures and temperatures when the cool cream touches the upper lip and the mouth is filled with hot whiskey-coffee.
>
> Remember: Irish coffee must be made with Irish whiskey and pure cream.

The Dunraven Arms

Warning—the bar in this thoroughly authentic old inn is habit-forming. It has been tastefully modernised so that the woody feel remains, and if you feel like adjourning for tea or a snack, there's a large and comfy lounge room. Sunny days can be enjoyed relaxing on the breezy patio out back.

Anascaul, Co. Kerry

Dan Foley's

Dan Foley's is one of Ireland's most famous and photogenic pubs. Its exterior is colourful to say the least, but not more so than its owner. Dan himself is a fascinating and highly entertaining man—a farmer, an expert on local history, adept in the fine art of conversation, and to top it all off, a magician.

If you like liqueurs, you'll be happy here—Dan stocks an amazing variety.

Ashford, Co. Limerick

Village Inn

A Tudor-style rural inn with loft stairs and thousands of pounds worth of antiques in every nook and cranny. Definitely worth a stop.

Ballybunion, Co. Kerry

If you're a bachelor and looking for an unusual experience, find out from the Irish Tourist Board what day in June will be Bachelor's Day in Ballybunion. Perhaps you'll be chosen the most eligible bachelor if you enter the contest. In any case, you'll enjoy the occasion and the contestants.

The Harty-Costello Pub

Owned by the chairman of the local development company, who is also a tourist's dream. He's a gentle raconteur, impish Kerryman and committed golfer. From him you can learn about the local mono-rail system, find out where to have a seaweed bath, or how to play the Ballybunion golf course, eighth best in the world (PGA ranking).

When you've had enough of the drink, refresh yourself down at the beach with its rugged cliffs, coves, and hidden caves.

Ballycanavan, Co. Waterford

Meades Bar

Meades is so cheery, it puts you in a good mood even if the day is stormy, and if there's sun, it's even better. The same family have run this delightful early eighteenth-century pub for 150 years and have had the wit to make the inevitable changes without disturbing the charm, personality, and character of the place.

The building reminded me of someone's dream cottage, with flower tubs at the door and pretty vines on the walls. Inside all is well-kept, shiny "tradition," with low ceilings, two small bars, open fires and interesting local artifacts.

On the flat roof of the kitchen, blending discreetly into the picture, is a beer garden and, out at the back, a barbeque area for summer fun.

The Meades are a friendly crew, and to add to the attraction of the place, they offer a good bar menu.

Ballydehob, Co. Cork

This little West Cork community is a thriving artists' and writers' colony of some renown and a haven for artistic international drop-outs (some famous) from all over the world. The shops and houses are painted different ice-cream pastel colours, and the shops contain some beautiful local crafts for you to bring home: batik, candles, pottery, paintings, sculpture, and hand-woven rugs. This is not the usual tourist mass-produced junk, but true art created by true artisans.

Levis

This pub has nothing to do with the famous brand of jeans, but has enough charm to have won renown all on its own. The charm is dispensed by the Levis (pronounced Lee-viss) sisters Julia and Nell, who have run this 150-year-old pub/grocery "since the year dot" and made it an institution in Ballydehob.

The bar has a delightfully symbiotic relationship with *Annie's*, a tiny restaurant across the street. Customers for the restaurant are sent to Levis as a kind of reception area, a congenial place to spend time waiting for a table or enjoying apéritifs.

Ballyvaughan, Co.Clare

Monks Pub

The Quay

A quayside, cottage-style pub modernised with great sensitivity by owners Bernadette and Michael Monks. There are several low ceilinged, white walled rooms with country furniture and open fires to gather around in winter. An intimate sort of atmosphere.

As if this isn't enough, Bernadette's home cooked bar food is a true taste treat. Try a seafood platter or a bowl of seafood chowder with brown bread and top your meal off with apple pie.

If you feel like a spot of conversation to go with your drink, there's a permanent fixture in the corner called Tom Collins (no, the cocktail was not named after him). Buy him a pint and he'll spin you some excellent yarns.

Ballyvourney, Co. Cork

The Mills Inn

Macroom-Killarney Road

Owned by the kindly Donal and Mary Scannell, this pub is a good stopping point on the Macroom-Killarney road. In fact it's is so multi-faceted you'll probably want to spend a little time here. The pub, established 1775, is on the grounds of what was once The Old Court House Castle, a hunting residence for George Coulthurst who also owned Blarney Castle. George's former happy hunting house has now crumbled to ruined walls and a tower on the green lawns of the pub's garden, adding just the perfect touch of melancholy romanticism.

Besides being a traditional style pub with log fires and oak beams, The Mills serves a good, complete and varied bar menu and has twelve bedrooms available upstairs for B & B.

There's a craft centre on the premises, but what particularly caught my fancy was Donal's fabulous museum of vintage cars, motorcycles and Irish farming memorabilia, all beautifully maintained and housed in a spanking clean stone outbuilding.

Care too, has been lavished on the large garden which is landscaped with exotic flowers and rare plant species.

Ask about traditional music and dance nights.

Bantry, Co. Cork

Encircled by gentle hills, Bantry dreams in the soft air. All manner of boats—spanking runabouts, Norwegian tunnies, royal yachts—bob at her quays. Bantry is a tourist centre, but somehow the large square open to the sea breeze seems to be able to accommodate the buses without loss of tranquillity.

Not to be missed: Bantry House, built in 1750 and filled with a fine collection of tapestries and other works of art. Wander in the lush Italian gardens, the setting for the jewel that is the house; then repair to a pub.

The Anchor Tavern

This typical pub of the area has a history that goes back 140 years and has been family-owned for the last three generations. The present family representative, William E. O'Donnell, is a firm believer in the fine old Irish pub tradition of using an artifact as a "talking point" to initiate a good flow of conversation. There's enough interesting nautical memorabilia here (including, yes, an old anchor) for days of discourse.

Birdhill, Limerick

Matt the Thresher

Dublin-Limerick road just outside Limerick

Matt's is a new pub unabashedly basing itself on old country traditions—red-tiled floors, country-kitchen furniture that blessedly is also comfortable, and chintz curtains. It's named in honour of a character in *Knocknagow*, a book which portrayed the proud traditions and values of a mythical Tipperary village. In the book, Matt was a professional thresher for the town.

Matt The Thresher has several irresistible things to recommend it: a good location, good food, and a pretty view of the Shannon Valley. There's a certain whimsicality to the place: with your food you'll get a note from Matt saying he hopes you like your meal.

The locals tolerate you very nicely, and the pub features a number of amusing, genuine artifacts.

Boher, Co. Limerick

P.A. McGrath's

Thatched pub with beautiful hearth and large back room lounge equipped with modified church panels and windows.

O'Neil's

Tiny, thatched authentic eighteenth-century "kitchen" pub with "Bothog" Bar and sugán furniture.

Bunratty Castle-Shannon Airport Vicinity

Durty Nellie's

Only seven miles (11 km) from Shannon Airport on the Limerick road, is Durty Nellie's, a ramshackle cottage with a thatched roof, sitting like some outrageous upstart at the foot of the monolithic Bunratty Castle. The pub is very famous, and is nearly always "packed out" cheek by jowl. The fact that it has been somewhat commercialised is no matter—the place is sheer fun.

It is a warren of small rooms, little bars, cosy inglenook seats and "courtin' corners." The walls are covered with historical artifacts, portraits of martyrs, statesmen, and their writings. Look at the walls for a short course in Irish history.

Durty Nellie's is borderline "twee" (self-consciously quaint), but manages not to fall on the wrong side of the border. The furniture and setting, in keeping with a tavern of the seventeenth-century, are somehow truly charming.

The downstairs is always crowded to bursting with jolly people, and the ensuing din is interlaced with the strains of impromptu music. You can addle yourself with a combination of Guinness and music by straddling the doorway between two rooms and attempting to listen to the music in each.

When you grow tired of the noise and smoke, take your pint and sit outside on the small veranda, or wander a few feet to the stone bridge that arches over the Shannon. I can't guarantee it, but one of the romantic high points of your Irish pub crawl just might be standing on the bridge with the moon rising over the river and Bunratty Castle, floodlit and imposing on your left. Sounds of laughter and music float out of the windows of the pub. The air is soft and still and evening birds swoop over all.

One of the most inspired aspects of the out-of-town Irish pub is the free flow between indoors and out. To emerge from the talk and dim cramp into the mellow smells and sights of an Irish evening is to delight the heart. Then, after dawdling in the luminous hush, you can duck back in for another round.

Caherdaniel, Co. Kerry

Caherdaniel is a peaceful retreat on the famous Ring of Kerry route, which brings you around the entire coast of Iveragh. It is situated near the shore of Derrynane Bay, where hillsides patterned with fields "the forty shades of green" slip gently to the water's edge.

Nearby is the haunting hermitage of St Crohane, hewn entirely from solid rock, as well as an ancient stone fort, every stone put into position without benefit of mortar of any kind.

Also in the vicinity is Derrynane House, the restored home of Daniel O'Connell, "the Liberator."

An Piobaire Dall (The Blind Piper)

Run by John Fitzgerald, who was described to me as, "a radical man; delightful, unconventional, and still not without 'the Blarney' and the innate knowledge of when and how to apply it."

It's a lovely, plain pub with decent food. Music and set dancing are a regular feature here.

Freddy's

Whether it be a pound of spuds or a bit of craic you're after, Freddy's will cater to you. At the front is a shop carrying practically everything and at the rear, through swinging doors, a bar and tables for a pint of porter.

If you grab a seat in the corner early on a Sunday morning, you are likely to overhear conversations ranging from sheep prices on the Beara peninsula to the latest anti-nuke demonstrations.

The ceilings are very low, giving the place a cosy feel. Freddy presides over the solid oak bar, opening the back door sometimes to let the flow of smoke out.

The toilets are located at the other side of an open courtyard, so you get a tan or double pneumonia, depending on the weather.

Note: Freddy himself is a direct descendant of Daniel O'Connell.

Cahirciveen, Co. Kerry

The ends of peninsulas seem to produce a feeling of loneliness and wind-washed clarity that nourishes the brain and stimulates the sense of wonder. Technology and politics don't make it out to the ends of the earth, and the people live in simple ways that reflect this welcome absence.

Cahirciveen is one such town, situated far out on the Iveragh peninsula at the foot of Bantee Mountain, overlooking the sea and Valentia Island (particularly popular with deep-sea anglers). In the summer, a number of artists and art students come here to paint, attracted by the beauty and the presence of an art school.

The Anchor

Paddy and Pauline Maguire have run this tiny place for many years and are known to discerning people all over Ireland. I first heard about The Anchor from the Irish writer and raconteur Ben Kiely, who listed it as a particular favourite.

The shops and houses that line the main street of an Irish town seem to have grown there, so naturally do they blend with their surroundings, forming a unity with street, hills, and sky. In one of these houses that make up the main street of Cahirciveen is The Anchor, a tiny, cluttered shop/bar. The day I arrived, Pauline, a small, salt-and-peppery woman, served me over the worn counter-bar in the dark little front room. She chatted easily, her sharp eyes taking me in all the while. From a curtained door came the sounds of television. "Come in," she said, inviting me through the curtain.

Several elderly men with pints by their sides were sitting in a living room watching the TV with rapt attention. The International Equestrian Jumping Competition was being televised from Germany. Ireland's entry, Eddie Macken, had been a previous champion on a horse named Kerry Gold, and the talk was about his chances of winning again.

Everyone in the room was immersed in the elegant images of formal perfection, of unity between horse and rider, that were reaching into the little back room all the way from Germany.

I looked around. It is somehow extraordinary to find yourself doing your official drinking in the living room of a perfect stranger —even in Ireland. It's not unusual to an Irishman, though. The custom dates back to the days of illegal poteen, and though growing fewer by the year, places like The Anchor can still be found in the countryside.

The room was furnished with comfortable, faded old chairs and a nice old sofa. There were several tables with oilcloth coverings, pictures of children in First Communion dress and people in wedding clothes, together with an amazing number of odd items hanging from the ceiling, such as woven baskets from Trinidad, mounted fish and dolls.

Pauline refreshed my drink, and we watched the contest in a silence interspersed with small bursts of congenial talk. The silvery sunlight of the late Irish afternoon moved across the room, and I wished I could stay forever. It was like visiting a favourite aunt.

The Point Bar

This is a beautiful place for a pub, or for any building for that matter. The Point overlooks Valentia Island and harbour and has been modernised discreetly so as to maintain an aura of simple and uncluttered authenticity. And heaven knows it's an authentic enough place—the pub has been passed down in the same family for 10 generations. If you think of time in terms of grandfathers, as I like to do, that would mean it's about a three grandfather pub.

Michael and Bridie O'Neill serve good bar food dishes and ultra-fresh fish and seafood prepared with simple wholesomeness. On fine days, it's great to eat and drink on the little patio and gaze past the old Great Southern & Western Railway terminal, on out to the open sea.

Cashel, Co. Tipperary

The Cashel Palace Hotel

You can stop here as a sort of homage to Arthur Guinness, the founder of the house of Guinness. The hotel was originally an archbishop's palace, and Arthur Guinness' father was the steward to the bishop. As a young man, Arthur planted hops here and made his first porter.

There's a very pleasant stone-floored bar downstairs and "buttery" type of restaurant with an open fire. Hot and cold food, fish dishes, soups and pies are the bar food specialities which, though not cheap, are quite good. I wonder what the bishop would think, not only of his protégé Arthur, but of all the people who now enjoy stopping in his former domain.

T.F. MEANEY'S

Conveniently situated on the main street, Meaney's is a handy place to stop for sandwiches and soup on the Dublin-Cork route. It's a pub with a character all its own: interesting red and turquoise paint-work, leaded windows, and a diverting collection of pewter mugs and plates, whiskey jars, bottles and jugs.

Meaney's is known too, for its traditional music. The scheduled evenings for music are Friday and Sunday (Wednesday too, in the summer). Impromptu sessions erupt all the time, and if you come bearing an instrument, you'll find you're very welcome to join in.

CASTLETOWNBERE, CO. CORK

> All around are the wild greys and greens of West Cork; the hundred islands of Roaringwater Bay in a flecked sea that for weeks has been unaccountably blue. Under this crazy sunshine it is like an unnaturally fertilized Greece . . . You can identify visitors by the fact that they alone wear native jerseys and Irish homespun (but) for some reason (this) seems more sympathetic here than anywhere else.
>
> *James Cameron*

The peninsulas of southwest Ireland reach into the sea like the paw of a bear reaching for a fish. Oddly, one of the wildest and most romantic of these peninsulas is called Beara. At the tip of this jumble of misty mountain-forest lies the town of Castletownbere.

It was in driving to this sleepy fishing village that I received a lesson in Irish time. At the top of one of the mountain passes beside a rocky waterfall, my car, after a few dispiriting thumpety-thumps, limped to a halt, sighed, settled, and let all the air out of the punctured left front tyre. I hitch-hiked to the nearest garage, sitting curled around my tyre in the back seat of a Renault, a feat worthy of the Incredible Rubber Man.

The garageman's verdict was that the tyre would be ready in half an hour. An hour later I inquired. He suggested a nice place down the road for a "cuppa" or a pint. Another half an hour and I began to frown, in spite of the lovely landscape I found myself in. After more delay, I became what used to be described as wroth.

The man eyed me with a calm twinkle. "Sure, and what'll the world be without ye when yer gone?" he said. I deflated in a fine imitation of my tyre. In Ireland no one hurries and time in truly relative; it is the broth in which events are savoured.

MacCarthy's

MacCarthy's is an archetypal Irish country pub—the kind of place that will make you think you've landed in a dream. In the front is a grocery store that provides for the trawlers docked in the harbour, and a snug. But this is no ordinary snug. It was once used as a match making booth, a private and neutral place for the match-maker to meet the parents of the bride and groom to discuss marriage terms (if only snugs could talk, I'm sure we'd hear some great tales). The back bar is well-known for its dart games and spontaneous music sessions.

O'Donaghue's

Main Square

Wide and sun-drenched, Main Square is bordered at one end by a pier and at the other sides by higgledy-piggledy pastel houses.

O'Donaghue's is an unprepossessing, typical, dark old pub; but the feeling is friendly, and you can't beat the location.

Among the fishermen who live and work in Castletownbere are many transplanted Dutch and English people. Tourism, however, is not that apparent here, and in O'Donaghue's you'll find mainly locals and the odd, sturdily booted student with his faithful knapsack.

Have a pint and then go to view the ruins of Dunboy Castle, which stands on a promontory with the Atlantic spreading before it. At one time it belonged to a powerful Irish prince, O'Sullivan Beare.

An ally of the Great O'Neill, he too went down to gallant defeat in the battle of Kinsale, the struggle that marked the end of Celtic-Norman Ireland.

Next to the stump of Dunboy Castle is the fire-gutted ruin of Puxley Hall, looking like the cover of a Gothic paperback romance.

Castletownshend, Co. Cork

Castletownshend is a particularly pretty Irish village with a steeply inclined street that charmingly enough sports an oak tree right in the middle. The large oak serves two purposes: as a delight, and as a leafy barrier to buses bearing hordes of tourists.

Mary Ann's Bar

Mary Ann's is a 150-year-old pub now in the capable hands of Fergus and Patricia O' Mahoney. It is low ceilinged, small and cosy, just the place to be on a rainy day. When the mist clears, lunch and drinks are served in a back garden under a shady grape arbor. Mary Ann's has won national acclaim for its excellent bar food (home-made soups, crab cocktail, sandwiches, steaks, salads and even oysters when available). If you'd like to start with drinks in the pub and then graduate to a more elaborate diner, just go upstairs to *The Contented Sole*, the restaurant where Patricia's good home cooking is earning her even more well deserved accolades.

The pub's clientele is a mixture of locals and low-key summer people. There is a large billiard table, and a dartboard in a back room, which is popular with the locals. When the occasion warrants, the billiard table gives way to a dance floor for local shindigs.

Cork City

The Bells of Shandon

With deep affection,
And recollection,
I often think of
Those Shandon bells

Whose sounds so wild would,
In the days of childhood,
Fling around my cradle
Their magic spells.

On this I ponder
Where'ere I wander,
And thus grow fonder,
Sweet Cork of thee;
With thy bells of Shandon,
That sounds so grand on
The pleasant waters
Of the River Lee.

Francis Sylvester Mahony

The capital of Munster is the city of Cork, the Republic of Ireland's "second city," but to the Corkman there is not even a remote question of comparison with Dublin—"Rebel" Cork is quite simply superior.

Cork is called "rebel" because the rugged individualism of her natives embraces not only personality and style but also historical stance. Throughout the trials of centuries, the people of Cork staunchly remained true products of Erin, and conquering powers were soon assimilated, any allegiance to them being at best superficial.

The town of Cork is picturesquely situated clasped between the arms of the River Lee and clinging to the surrounding hilltops. Yet in spite of its quaint quays and towers, the Republic's highly important Atlantic seaport is a commercial nexus, the export centre for the agricultural produce of the south.

There is a businesslike atmosphere about the main streets of Cork as the town hustles to impress its new aggressive image as a rising modern centre of industry and host to a gaggle of foreign manufacturers.

In spite of all this emphasis on trade, Cork maintains a proud tradition of support for the arts: ballet, theatre, art, and music. The

Cork Film Festival has somehow navigated the rocky shoals of Irish censorship, and international stars and directors mingle in the pubs with the sportsmen and yachting enthusiasts who are an ever-present phenomenon.

This tough, mercantile, yet poetic place has yielded a rich crop of writers: Sean O'Faolain, Frank O'Connor, and Daniel Corkery are all native sons whose work will reward the reader with special insight into the nature of life—universal, Irish and Corkonian.

An Spailpin Fanac
28/29 South Main Street
This is a soothing pub recently renovated, predominantly in natural earth tones to go with low ceilings, brick walls and a simple wooden bar with woven rush seats. The bar food is lovely and wholesome—try the traditional bacon and cabbage or the cornbeef and veggie platter, for instance.

The name, by the way, translates roughly as "the jobbing traveller," and I think you should ask the very friendly proprietor about why he chose it and what it means.

Dan Lowrey's Seafood Tavern
13 MacCurtain Street
Here's a small pub (two rooms, one with an open fire) that is perfect for a rendezvous. The pub is directly across from the comfortably fashionable Issacs Restaurant, and has been renovated with great respect for its origins as a pub in 1875—wooden floor, gorgeous mahogany bar with unusual shelving and antique bevelled mirrors, and the pièce de résistance, stained-glass windows that come from Kilkenny Cathedral.

The bar food is an above-average selection of soups, salads, seafood and meat platters.

The Hi-Bi
Corner of Winthrop and Plunkett St
Above Minahan Chemists
The Hi-Bi is an affectionate nickname, a play on the word Hibernian which is the pub's more formal moniker. Well hidden at the top of an old, linoleum-floored staircase, this tiny place can be packed out with a real Cork crowd, a mixed bunch of working types, artists, writers, writers manqués, "beautiful" people and just plain folks.

As soon as I entered, I was accosted by a gentleman in a rumpled white linen suit with a rosebud in his lapel. It was immediately quite obvious to me that he had already been there for several hours. When I told him I was writing a pub guide he was horrified.

"Don't you dare include this bar," he told me severely, "you'll ruin it."

After thinking the matter over, I decided I would include it after all, but with the caveat that it's not for everyone. It's a little dingy as well as a tight fit when the after-work hordes invade, but then again, it's a charming and welcoming place to stop by in the daytime (not lunch), when there's practically no one there and you can sit peacefully in front of a small grate with a fire warming your toot-sies and a copy of the *Cork Examiner* in your lap.

Whatever you do, however, don't mention this book when you come in, especially not if you see a man in a white linen suit with a rosebud boutonnière.

THE LONG VALLEY BAR/THE HAYLOFT LOUNGE BAR
10 Winthrop St

From the moment I entered the Long Valley I loved it. To the right of the wood panelled entrance hallway is a built-in display case with bevelled glass windows exhibiting bottles of wine, vodka, whiskey, scotch and various liqueurs as well as small, cut crystal glasses. To the left is a snug with etched glass windows and chased silver door-knobs—real quality workmanship in a pub that's been entertaining Cork folk since 1842. All this before you have even walked into the bar itself.

The Long Valley could just as well be called the Long Room. It's one of those pubs that's narrow and deep with an endless bar and wooden tables, chairs and benches that run along the opposite wall. Behind the bar is a huge old stove steaming with good things to eat. Staff dressed in white butcher coats supply the lively, predominantly thirty-something crowd with a continuous stream of hunky, deli-type sandwiches of all sorts, made to order on delicious slabs of home-baked brown bread. There's a great feeling of cheerful bustle here, as though you've wandered into a convivial party in someone's home.

The historic photos on the wall are fun too—I particularly liked the one of a ship in full sail that hangs right above the stove.

The upstairs lounge called The Hayloft is quieter, a place where you can retreat from the merrymaking to sit at pine tables.

The spirit of the Long Valley is embodied in its proprietors, the delightfully eccentric Rita and Humphrey Moynihan, a couple now in their mid seventies, who are almost as famous in Cork as their pub.

Humphrey, a spry and slender fella with observant eyes, took me into the little upstairs kitchen so we could chat quietly. We wedged our chairs in between the sink and fridge and there, with a pint in one hand and shelves of kitchen staples above our heads, I was royally entertained.

Humphrey told me a great many things over the next hour. All of the information was embroidered with copious asides and delivered in a kind of mesmerising tone that reminded me of a shanachie.

Among a variety of other things, I learned that he had been an economics teacher in a school in Rathmines until 1927, when he inherited the pub from his father, a Cork draper who had once done a turn in London as a Saville Row tailor.

"When the pub first opened in 1842," he told me, "Cork had 400 pubs of which only 70 were independently owned by the occupants. The rest were tithe houses owned by the local breweries who, in those days, made very inferior stout compared to Guinness. Today those same breweries are massive. One of them is owned by Heinekens and the other by Fosters and they make extraordinarily good black porter.

"Now, the origin of porter or stout comes from the dockers and porters in London who were mostly of Irish Catholic stock. They were very poorly paid and could afford only the cheapest of beer, so they put roasted barley in it to cover up the bad taste. And that drink became known as 'porter.'

"Now then, Guinness in Dublin began to make a strong version of that drink, and the common word for strong in the last century and the century before that was stout, so that's how come Guinness's drink became known as 'stout' porter.

"I knew all about the old way of making black beer or stout, but the modern way is you just sit down at the computer and it's all a mixture of chemicals. The old-fashioned way you'd be washing out the vats and there'd be rats and everything, but that's all gone now."

At one point I asked Humphrey why his bar staff wore white coats.

"Oh yes, well," he nodded and grinned, "I saw a New York bar on the television, where they all wore the white coats with black aprons. I thought it looked good. It's a Victorian custom — goes with an old-fashioned bar. People like it."

I liked it too — in fact I loved the entire pub and long may Humphrey and Rita thrive.

When you go to the Long Valley say hello to Humphrey and ask to see the wonderful guest book which he started in 1947. It's full of cartoons, drawings, photos and comments like "The moving finger writes and having written moves on. I hope it doesn't write or move on too fast."

The Oyster Tavern

Market Lane off Patrick Street

A famous and elegant tavern is The Oyster Tavern, carpeted and polished, with old prints on the wall, cut glass and heavy wooden chairs. Prior to 1828, one Wicklow Stokes held the premises under lease from Edward Barrett, a publican, and Richard Fitzgerald, a brewer.

There are a number of small dining salons, a fireplace, main room, and bar. Needless to say, oysters are the stars of the menu with other types of seafood following close behind.

Rearden's

Washington Street

Rearden's is a newly reborn pub on an old site, a charming place for a delicious, inexpensive meal along with your pint. There are two good-sized rooms and the décor is stone and wood, with wooden barrels set into the walls. The long bar is made of shiny but not obtrusive pine supported on a base of kegs. The ceiling is beamed, and a pleasant atmosphere is created with rush baskets, old bottles, etc..

I sat in one of the roomy booths and enjoyed well-cooked plaice, a fish I had not been acquainted with previously. "You've got a nice plaice here," I said to the waitress, unable to resist the pun. Quick as a flash the waitress parried with, "That's kind of a fishy compliment, isn't it?" In Cork no one minds the incorrigible punster.

An additional note on the pubs of Cork: the game of darts is a highly esteemed form of recreation here, and you'll find a number of clubs and teams in heavy competition all over town.

Reidy's Wine Vaults

Lancaster Place Western Road

Just opposite Jury's Hotel is this entertaining pub stylishly converted from a wine warehouse. Special features: high vaulted ceilings, a minstrel gallery, traditional black and white tiled floor and a massive mahogany Victorian bar to end Victorian bars, complete with London clock and bevelled mirrors. Excellent bar food with a blackboard menu of fresh daily choices. Home baking.

Bar Food: 10.30 a.m.–9.30 p.m.

Also under Reidy management is The Château on Patrick Street, a good central Cork lunch stop.

The Vineyard

The Vineyard is about 200 years old and has been renovated with great taste and style. It is a large, rambling pub with two snugs and the traditional partitions along the bar; the centre of the room is capped with a superbly light, greenhouse-like glass ceiling raised on a wooden base. This bit of inspired architecture lends an airy quality to the whole, which is fortunate, as the place is almost always dense with smoke and people.

The Vineyard caters to a mixed group of the young and the businessman. It is a particular favourite of the rugby crowd, both fans and players. After a few hours in The Vineyard you will soon understand why the city of Cork has such a reputation for being sports-mad; much of the talk revolves around sports events, sports figures, sports stories, and even conversation itself is treated as a sport.

The people are exceptionally friendly and spontaneous, and I found myself invited to a dance down the road in a matter of moments. I couldn't go, having to keep a previous appointment. I took a taxi, and the driver said to me in his flat Cork accent, "Yiss, yiss, a nice girl like you requires a nice night life." It was raining; we drove along past dripping trees. An old man sat on a bench waiting for the bus.

DINGLE, CO. KERRY

O Gaelic, most sweet and soft of sound
Swift, robust, as the waves of the sea,
Trodden and trampled, despised by all -
That you live is a wonder to me!

Peadar O'Doirnin

Dingle Peninsula stretches thirty spectacular miles (48 km) into the Atlantic. Like Beara it is wild and mystical, but Dingle is more barren and possesses a greater sense of timeless prehistory. Here language is old, too—this is the Gaeltacht, the area where Gaelic is still spoken and taught.

Great cliffs fall hundreds of feet to the sea, vistas of light-blessed grandeur unfold before you as you travel the narrow coast roads. One can wander with J.M. Synge:

> I walked up this morning along the slope from the east to the top of Sybil Head, where one comes out suddenly on the brow of a cliff with a straight fall of many hundreds of feet into the sea. It is a place of indescribable grandeur, where one can see Carrauntuohill and the Skelligs and Loop Head and the full sweep of the Atlantic, and over all, the wonderfully tender and searching light that is seen only in Kerry. Looking down the drop of five or six hundred feet, the height is so great that the gannets flying close over the sea look like white butterflies, and the choughs like flies fluttering behind them. One wonders in these places why anyone is left in Dublin, or London, or Paris, when it would be better, one would think, to live in a tent or hut with this magnificent sea and sky, and to breathe this wonderful air, which is like wine in one's teeth.

Ancient stone forts, clochâns and crosses abound, and myths hang in the air on the verge of becoming visible. Standing on the beach at Ventry, you can easily picture the events said to have taken place there: Daire Doon, the primeval King of the World, arriving in his colourful ships to conquer Ireland and meeting defeat on the beach at the hands of the giant Finn MacCool and his warriors, the Fianna.

Modern fables, too, have taken place on Dingle: *Ryan's Daughter* was filmed here, and an entire Irish village, Kirrary, built for it. After the film, the town was dismantled, but the experience lingers in the conversation of Dingle natives.

The mother goddess has always had a strong hold on the Kerry imagination, coming to them in many mystic guises: the Hag of Beara, the Sky Woman, and here in Dingle, the Fair Lady Banba, who dwells in the mountains of Slieve Mish. It is said that her influence generates a wild restlessness in these hills. So if it's primal nature and Celtic romance you're after, make your headquarters in Dingle and explore the peninsula.

An Droichead Beag (The Small Bridge)

Built on a bridge, this old style pub with stone floor, two ranges and many artifacts is owned and run by Maura Ferris (née Walsh). Maura and her assistant Aine are two lively Gaelic women with the gift of speaking real West Kerry Irish, and a lovely air of wit, charm and good humour.

A West Kerry crowd mixes here with cosmopolitans, and the place has earned a name for good music.

T. & G. Ashe

The Ashe family have distributed Guinness in west Kerry for generations and the pub has hosted diplomats, ministers, senators and rogues. Come here and you're sure to be regaled with a fund of stories, tall tales, and "secrets." You'll also hear some great Irish spoken.

Dick Mack's

Dingle is like a little world apart, and everyone in Ireland seems to love it. "Oh, *Dingle*," people say, voices filled with remembered pleasure or regret that they have not yet visited. The town's inhabitants are just as special as Dingle itself—an eclectic melange of local people, transplants from other parts of Ireland, and international "expats."

The place to go for an amusing introduction to the citizenry is Dick Mack's. The pub, a favourite with visitors and residents alike, has a delightfully split personality, being part restaurant, part pub and part leather goods shop. In 1900, Dick Mack "himself," ran the place as a pub and a shoemaker shop all in one, and the store is still there, featuring plenty of old stock as well as modern leatherware and "wellies."

Dick's son Oliver now runs the pub, creating an atmosphere of conviviality and fun.

On a typical evening the patrons might include Ena and Geraldine Keogh—Ena holding court on the piano and Geraldine (an artist who paints with both words and brush) just holding court. More than likely you would also find another artist, Jay Killian, formerly of Bristol, Massachusetts, whose canvases depicting local scenes decorate the walls of the pub.

Doyle's Townhouse

John Street

This is the place to go if you want mouthwatering bar food or a full meal. Lobster, the house speciality, is chosen from a tank in the bar. The menu features only the freshest of fare and the seafood is chosen daily from the fish landed in the Dingle boats.

In the last number of years, Doyle's has become one of Ireland's leading eating places and has received awards from top good food guides, the Irish Tourist Board "Award of Excellence" and the United Dominions Trust Endeavour Award.

An old kitchen range, súgán chairs, kitchen tables and the use of natural stone and wood combine to give Doyle's a cosy country atmosphere.

James Flahive

The Quay

There has been a fishing fleet moored at what is called Dingle Marina for centuries. The main street has always been called the Quay, and along it you will find the various shops necessary to support a fishing fleet. One such "shop" is Flahive, a second home to many a sailor.

Since it opened in 1897 it's been a tailor shop and pub, a grocery store and pub, and as of 1985, strictly a pub. The proprietors are James Flahive and his wife Peggy, "the lady of the house." They live above the store with James' great aunt Ellen who is circa 106 years old, and as of this moment, still going strong. When Ellen is "in residence" she sits in the back room next to a stove that is positively magical. Purchased in 1908 from the catalogue of John Atkins and Co. Ltd Scotland, the highly polished chromium stove is in use every day. It's hard to believe that something so beautiful and so old can look so sparklingly new and function so smoothly.

There are no plans to change anything at Flahive's including the loo which is out in the back yard and open to the elements. Every Saturday night there's a weekly card game in the back room, and when appropriate the fire is lit.

An amusing note: James' mother-in-law and actor Gregory Peck's mother are cousins and photos of Mr Peck chumming around with various members of the family are on display everywhere, as are pictures of other distinguished visitors. The star photo in the "gallery" however, is definitely Fungie, Dingle Bay's resident dolphin.

Mairead De Barres

The Quay

Mairead and her husband Pat Leahy each left thriving careers in broadcast journalism at RTE (she a newscaster, he a cameraman), to bring their love of Irish language and lore to pier-side Dingle. They have a beautifully plain pub, good food at very reasonable prices, and when Mairead speaks Gaelic I can hear echoes of all the voices of her lineage.

The pub has a nice view of the harbour home of Fungie, Dingle's much adored dolphin.

The Mall

The Mall, undoubtedly the tiniest pub in Dingle, is owned by Madge Barret, a woman with what might very well be one of the biggest hearts in town. The Mall has been passed down in Madge's family for 180 years and when she retires, her son James (now a lobster fisherman), will carry on the tradition.

Madge is the only person working in the pub, and you'll love her, but if you're more than 6 feet (1.8 m) tall you won't be able to stand up straight and will have to remain seated on your bar stool.

Madge lives above the pub and in addition to her quarters, there are two B & B rooms available. Call well in advance to book them: 066 51770.

O'Flaherty's

Dingle is a small fishing and local merchant's town (pop. 1,000) on the sea surrounded on three sides by hills. Across from the police station, beside the sea, is O'Flaherty's, one large barnlike room with a long bar on one side and a raised platform for musicians on the other. Fergus O'Flaherty, the pub's owner, is a very fine musician, a master of the tin whistle, flute, accordion, banjo and more than likely any other instrument you'd care to imagine.

Fergus plays here himself, and foot tapping, inspiring traditional music takes over nightly from May to September, whether impromptu or scheduled.

If you want a bodhrán (Irish goatskin drum) specially made and hand-painted for you, this is the place to ask about it.

The pub is around 150 years old, with red-timbered walls and the bar-counter is high enough that, as a regular confided to me, "when ya put yer elbows down, the drink rushes to yer head faster." Photographs, old advertisements, and poetry are pinned up on rough walls, and it's enjoyable to wander around, pint in hand, reading.

You'll always find a hearty welcome at O'Flaherty's, especially in

August at the time of the annual Curragh races, when the talk is either about the day's race or the oyster catch. The crowd is made up of Dingle fishermen and local people, students of the Gaelic language, tourists, and a variety of elegant folk "roughing it"—writers, intellectuals, politicians, and businessmen all fleeing the rigours of their lives. Many have remote houses to which they retire, coming out in the evening to gather in the conviviality generated at O'Flaherty's.

Doolin, Co. Clare

O'Connor's

O'Connor's has earned an international reputation as a mecca for traditional music. The place has been in the O'Connor family since 1832, and the present Mr O'Connor is very friendly. Five families, he told me, still live in Doolin Cove where they survive by carrying on the tradition of lobster fishing.

In the front is the usual small Irish grocery store with a tiny counter and shelves crammed with everything from Galtee cheese to gloves.

The extensions in the back have been added on to over the years. The main room is blessed with a fireplace for cold, misty days, and on the walls are dozens of photographs of the musicians who play here, of fishermen, of Irish faces and Irish life.

The music is not organised—the sessions are spontaneous, occurring night and day, whenever the musicians choose to drop in. Sandwiches and coffee are available (besides pints), but no one minds if you go out front, buy your bit of cheese, ham and tomatoes and eat your purchase then and there at one of the tables. The crowd is local-international; rucksacks and young faces abound. It's great craic—and you can sing along.

Dromineer, nr Nenagh, Co. Tipperary

Sail Inn

Here's a pub right on Lough Derg that was recommended to me by the writer Hugh Leonard who says: "The pub is part of a splendid inn and restaurant run by a daunting English lady—or Lady, rather, since she is titled. I myself had the honour of declaring the new bar open, and the view from its balcony is enchanting."

The Whiskey Still
On grassy lawns abutting the harbour are two rough-plastered, pebble dash cottages which are joined together. This siamese-twins type pub has two bars and two fireplaces, Irish traditional music cassettes softly playing, and decent food gently priced.

Dunmore East, Co. Waterford

The Ship
Many in Ireland have heard of this well-located roadside pub and restaurant because it nicely combines outstandingly good local seafood dishes and a relaxed, informal atmosphere for quaffing a pint. The front bar is pleasantly nautical, dimly lit and decorated in dark wood. The bar space flows easily into a dining area outfitted with unusual furniture, which though cunningly fashioned from barrels, is still comfortable.

There's a balmy, roadside patio for casual summer meals.

Dunquin, Co. Kerry

Kruger's Inn
Off Slea Head at the tip of Dingle Peninsula lie the Blasket Islands. Beyond, according to Celtic fable, is Tir-na-nóg, land of perpetual youth, the Beyond Otherworld. Actually, what lay beyond the Blaskets *was* another world—America. The Blasket Islands are the most western lands in Europe.

In 1953, life on these windswept stones became untenable for the few who still clung to them, and the last inhabitants were moved to the mainland. Many settled in Dunquin.

You'll probably find some of these islanders in Kruger's, a fine place for the dance and the singsong and, if you're lucky, the memory or tale well told. Or perhaps you'll get a genuine Irish viewpoint on those who played at being Irish — the crew and cast of *Ryan's Daughter* used to come to Kruger's for rest and rehabilitation.

Ennis, Co. Clare

The Cloister

Abbey Street

Here's a pub that has everything: history, ambience, good cheer and bar food that has earned the pub a reputation that goes beyond local perimeters.

The pub is quite literally a part of Irish history, built right into the walls and garden of a thirteenth-century Franciscan friary with windows that overlook the friary and its lawns, fabulously green even to the eye of an Irish person well acquainted with the phenomenon of emerald-like grass.

Fire-warm and shadowy in winter, the pub expands in the summer to include a pretty patio garden.

Fethard, Co. Tipperary

McCarthy's

Here's a very old, family-owned hotel and pub in horse breeding stud country, the home of good conversation and lively friends. Authentic wooden decor.

Glin, Co. Limerick

Conway's

A comfortable, clean pub and ex hotel that dates back to the eighteenth century and is owned by great conversationalists with a wealth of lore about the Shannon area and the fabled Knights of Glin.

A friend comments on Conway's: "If ever I'm passing I don't. John and Christine are gorgeous. She's a wonderful, brazen headed woman (red hair) and he's the kind will stop everything and go out in a boat with you if you want."

Haughnessy's

Unchanged, true "olde worlde" pub owned by "the Captain," an ex British army eccentric with a fund of stories and opinions. Featured by *Fortune Magazine.*

Kenmare, Templenoe, Co. Kerry

Pat Spillane's

Owned by a local teacher, all Ireland medallist and eight times Carroll's all star, this pub overlooks a remote bay where locals enjoy occasional outdoor set-dancing, if they are not inside admiring their celebrated compatriot's awards.

Killaloe-Ballina, Co. Clare

Goosers

People from practically every county kept recommending Goosers to me and, as it turns out, with good reason. This traditional pub, just below Lough Derg at the Shannon's widest point, offers exceptionally good food, characterful ambience, music and a view of the river sports.

There are several intimate bar spaces for you to chose from, and you can relax into the cheery atmosphere created by rustic furniture and a carefully selected assortment of antique bric-à-brac.

The edibles vary from a snack to a three course blackboard menu, but offerings are uniformly delicious.

Seafood and traditional fare are the pub's strengths.

Irish Molly's

A quality new pub done in the old style, on the banks of the Shannon. Run by a totally eccentric Englishman with a million opinions. Have fun.

Killarney, Co. Kerry

For many people, Kerry is like the geographical crock of gold at the end of Ireland's rainbow, for it boasts the three large and jagged peninsulas of Beara, Iveragh, and Dingle—those misty regions of ancient Celtic magic.

The most travelled of the three, Iveragh, takes you on the first leg of the famous "Ring of Kerry," a stretch of road that offers rare and awe-inspiring vistas. At the base of Iveragh lies that hive of tourist activity, Killarney.

The town itself is a traffic jam in the summer, and its natives are well versed in dispensing professional Irish charm. It is an expensive place geared to the busloads of tourists that are disgorged in front of the Great Southern Hotel.

The vale of Killarney, however, in which the town nestles, is so beautiful that Brendan Behan once said, "even an ad man would be ashamed to eulogise it."

Three main lakes occupy a broad valley stretching south between the mountains. These lakes are surrounded by luxuriant woods of oak, arbutus, birch, holly, and mountain ash. The ground is soft with moss and the air fragrant with flowery freshness. Cars are barred from the many ferny trails, so take a rewarding hike or hire a "jarvey" (horse and old-fashioned jaunting car), left over from the days when the Victorians discovered Killarney and painted and poeticised it into world popularity.

Like as not, the jarvey driver will be giving plenty of blarney for tourist consumption (a favourite trick: "Ah, and there's one of the wee folk right over there under that bush—ah, ya just missed him"), but take him in along with the scenery.

KATE KEARNEY'S
Gap of Dunloe
About 5 miles (8 km) outside Killarney
Here you can take refreshment at the same cottage where once the elegantly attired Victorians sipped illegal poteen prepared for them by Kate herself. Then, fortified, you will be ready for the Ice Age miracles of the Gap of Dunloe. All cars are left behind and you descend into this cleft in the earth on foot or by pony trap.

Transferring to a boat, you are then treated to a romantic's fantasy come true as you slide along the lakes, great boulders to either side. You pass places with names like "The Devil's Punchbowl" and "The Eagles' Nest," said to be the last refuge of the Irish eagle.

There are a number of other sights in this area, but a real *must* is Muckross. A nineteenth-century manor house on the middle lake, set in subtropical gardens, the trails lead you through masses of rhododendrons and azaleas, as well as water, woodland, and rock gardens.

After these pleasures, perhaps you can brave the town for a jar or a pint.

Molly D'Arcy's

This prize winning, newly thatched pub at the gates of Muckross National Park is part of a hotel owned by a car magnate, who named the place after his mother.

Features include a huge bar, public phones in what were confession boxes salvaged from a monastery, a whiskey corner and a patron's "Mug Club."

The confession box phones give you a chance for a really "private" conversation, and the hotel itself has attractive rooms with a fresh décor including Laura Ashley prints and Stephen Pearce lamps.

Kinsale, Co. Cork

Kinsale has all the charm of a seaport that technology has passed by. The town is terraced into the slope of Compass Hill with an almost Mediterranean charm, its narrow winding lanes bordered by a fine collection of Georgian houses. There are several cliff walks that are as wild and haunting as anything you can imagine. The stone embattlements of old Fort Charles afford a magical view of the town and a camper's paradise if you want to spend a night or two under the stars.

Kinsale has also become a kind of sub-rosa Irish Riviera, attracting in a low-key way a fashionable crowd both domestic and international. When I was visiting, President Mary Robinson was in town entertaining the Ambassador from Portugal. Much to everyone's delight and approval, she had her hair coiffed for the occasion at the shop of a local hairdresser. The resultant traffic jam was tolerated with great good cheer.

Kinsales's famous boatyards and ideal harbour play host to yachts and sailing vessels of all kinds and all flags, and the town has also become a focal point for the best in Irish culinary art. Good restaurants abound and the yearly Kinsale Gourmet Festival is a week long culinary extravaganza. Every two years Kinsale also hosts an international gourmet cooking competition appropriately called the International Food Forum. Surprisingly, there aren't that many fat people in Kinsale—perhaps there's something special in the sea air that keeps you thin.

The Blue Haven

Pearse Street

The bar at the Blue Haven Hotel has a wide range of imaginative bar food including a mixed bean curry served with chutney, poppadoms and savoury rice, but what especially caught my fancy is the conservatory—a pretty glassed-in patio that opens into a little flowery garden. It's a bright place to go on a drizzly day.

The Bulman

Waterfront

Twilight at The Bulman is a special treat. The 200-year-old pub, situated about a mile along the harbour in the direction of Fort Charles, is right on the quay: you can wander out with your pint and watch the gulls turn iridescent in the sunset and listen to the gentle knocking of waves against the stone wharf.

Inside the small pub is a sweatered and rubber-booted bunch, most of whom know each other. You can't tell the fishermen from the yachtsmen here, and the American gone native is hard to tell from the Canadian who has settled here to earn his keep at fishing. There is a lot of good-natured ribbing about national quirks.

The foreigners in Kinsale are either old and rich or young and eccentric. The night I visited The Bulman, I met the younger crowd: two Australians, a Frenchman, a German, an Englishman, and an American. I also met an entire contingent of rather whimsical local people. It was a zany expatriate scene, and the American warned me not to stay over two days if I wanted to get away at all.

Main topics of conversation in Kinsale: boats, fishing, yachts, sailing, real estate (the Dutch and Germans have bought heavily in this area), and food.

Note: the bar serves excellent coffee. Owners Chris and Laurie have noticed that many people have begun to prefer non-alcoholic beverages in the daytime.

1601

Pearse Street

This centrally located, friendly and peaceable pub is paradoxically named after the date of a famous conflict—the battle of Kinsale. You can get a painless history lesson about it in an interesting and decorative presentation in the front lounge.

The pub is extremely popular with both locals and visitors and is split into coffee bar, pub and restaurant sections. The emphasis on a coffee bar reflects the fact that while people still like to go to pubs, they are, in fact, drinking less (though talking just as much). There's a piano bar and a small, intimate back room with a fireplace which seats only about 50 people.

The food is super-fresh, home-made, tasty and well-priced. What more do you want.

The Spaniard

High on Compass Hill, overlooking the sea, is a thatched and white-washed stone building with a sign depicting a dark and laughing cavalier—obviously the Spaniard in question. (The Irish have a special friendship with Spain dating back several centuries).

Out front amid the flowers are a few tables and benches, excellent for watching the sunset and meeting convivial strangers. Within, all is smoky-dim, low-ceilinged, and cosy. Built in the seventeenth century, the main room boasts a large fireplace. There are a number of adjoining rooms with small windows, rustic décor and some amusing local artifacts like a four foot salmon caught at Little Island in 1912.

This is a very friendly, amiable place to settle into and if you love music, you'll find sessions that include blues, jazz, and contemporary folk as well as well as Irish traditional.

Mary O'Toole's bar food is both simple and scrumptious, especially her version of that traditional standby, bacon and cabbage. Prices are reasonable.

For more details on music sessions call 021 772436.

The Spinnaker Scilly

If you want a waterfront pub with good bar food at really affordable prices this is your place. Done in nautical themes, flags of various boats on the ceiling, it's a lively, young person's pub.

Killorglin, Co. Kerry

Normally a quiet little town with twenty four pubs, Killorglin becomes a focal point for thousands of people once a year, in August. The occasion is Puck Fair, one of the last vestiges of pagan fertility rites in Europe. There's a legend that "Puck" commemorates an occasion when the stampeding of goats gave warning of the approach of English forces.

Puck Fair is a village street fair, a musical event, and an enthusiastic and sometimes overflowing celebration of life-energy. While the event *has* been much commercialised, its spirit survives. Be forewarned, however, of all the inconveniences of a small area inundated by a large crowd.

Reigning over all is the King of the Fair, the Puck, a fine male goat ensconced on a platform above the heads of the swirling crowd.

By late afternoon of "Gathering Day"—normally 10 August—the crowds are sparking with anticipation. The men of the town have returned from Macgillycuddy's Reeks, the magnificent range to the south, one of whose peaks, Carrauntuohill (the Left-Handed Reaping Hook), is the highest in Ireland. They have brought back unharmed the largest and handsomest he-goat they could find.

Accompanied by the enthusiastic crowd and a band of pipes, drums, and flutes, the Puck is taken to the town square and crowned by a young girl (the obligatory virgin). Decorated and beribboned, he is then raised by a pulley system to the top of a three-tiered 52-foot platform (hung with an enormous banner advertising Guinness), from which he will reign for the next three days.

When Puck reaches the top, the excited crowd bursts into dancing and celebration which will continue for the next three nights. At sunset of the third day (Scattering Day), the Puck is dethroned and set free, but the revelling continues till dawn.

Until fairly recently, Puck Fair had its sordid side too: there was drunkenness and brawling and the streets were filthy with manure from the horses and cattle brought to the fair. Now however, the town fathers have literally cleaned up the occasion, retaining the ebullience but creating a holiday atmosphere in which events of all sorts are planned—pub and street entertainment, family fun and river sporting events.

THE FISHERY

One of the new "old" pubs, this one is a thatched edifice housing "Rogha Gach Bia agus Thoga Gach Di" (the best of food and drink). It's a marvellous place fixed up in the old schoolhouse tradition, and run by Edso Crowley, a master of song and story, invention and improvisation.

THE OLD FORGE

Out of the mass of bars in Killorglin, The Old Forge is one of the most authentic, from the thatched roof to the used fishing net on the ceiling. It has a good-size bar, the ever-present lounge, and—surprise—a courtyard with two saunas.

Naturally, The Old Forge should receive your patronage, especially during Puck Fair, when a sauna is just the thing you need to keep you going.

Kilmoon, Co. Meath

The Snail Box

Four miles (6 km) North of Ashbourne on the N2

A comfortable, friendly, rural bar where a lively game of pool is the star attraction. Nice fires to lounge at in between games. The odd name comes from a historic local legal case. It seems that in the early 1800s, the pub's site was common land and a hedge schoolmaster settled there for a while. A local landlord took him to court to have him evicted but lost the case when the judge ruled that, "the snail and his box can settle where he chooses."

Lahinch, Co. Clare

The Corner Stone

Originally Hogan's House, this 125-year-old flagstone building stands proudly on Main Street in Lahinch. If you ask the friendly proprietor, Ray Conroy, he'll be glad to show you how he recently turned the bedroom and kitchen of the old house into the front bar, which now includes a fireplace with moose antlers over it.

The Corner Stone serves pub food, but also incorporates Pony Mac's Kitchen, which has a more extensive menu and a reputation for creating marvellous porter cake for over half a century.

June to September: traditional music every night. Winter: music on weekends only.

The Corner Stone also operates a small B & B. Phone: 065 81277.

The Nineteenth Hole

I discovered that Ireland is an enthusiastic place for golf and that much business is done out there on the greens. Lahinch has two golf courses and the Lahinch Gold course is a PGA rated championship course.

Hence the name of this pub, housed in a building over a century old. The floor is flagstone, the walls whitewashed and there is traditional music and a show nightly.

Spend an evening in Lahinch, and then early the next day (if you can face it) drive north a few miles along the coast road through the little fishing village of Lisacannor to the Cliffs of Moher, rising a dramatic 700 feet (213 m) from the sea. Take the windy, winding cliff walk to the lookout in O'Brien's Tower and "hang your head over, hear the wind blow." This lonely old tower is a romantic landmark, small as the human presence against the might of cliffs, sky and sea.

From this perch you can see the west coast from Kerry to Connemara. The famous Moher flagstones are quarried near here. In former times a bride's dowry often consisted of "Moher flags," which provided a floor for many a humble kitchen. This stone is still in great demand for flooring and fireplaces.

LIMERICK, CO. LIMERICK

Limerick cured ham and Limerick lace enjoy a worldwide reputation. The thousand-year-old city, located on the estuary of the Shannon, once drew Norse and English overlords; now it is a terminal for rail and sea traffic.

On Bridge Street is the Gerald Griffin Memorial School, formerly the old courthouse where the trial of John Scanlon took place for the murder of his wife, Ellen. He was defended by Daniel O'Connell, but even that great orator couldn't save him, and he was executed. The story of this love-murder inspired a young Limerick reporter to write a novel about it, *The Collegians*, which in turn became the basis for the famous Boucicault drama *The Colleen Bawn*. Almost every man, woman, and child in Ireland can tell you the story, and will, at the drop of a pint.

My friend Michael Crowley, now a Limerick resident, told me another "special" thing about the town. "Limerick is famous for its women," he informed me. "In the siege of Limerick in 1690, when the battle was all but lost, the women rallied behind the men, holding off the British forces long enough for the men to regroup and win. It was the women who turned the tide of history that day."

Michael smiled. "And of course Limerick women have a reputation for being very good looking. When I was a young man I used to come down from Dublin to meet them—to give truth to the legend, you see."

Nancy Blake's

Nancy presides here with a strong but kindly hand, and has for longer than anyone can tell me. The pub hasn't been changed for years. You can still see the way the lounge was converted from a living room sometime in the 1950s—the flock wall paper that was popular back then remains. For some reason, everyone likes to crowd in the narrow passageway between the lounge in the back and the bar in the front—maybe that's why another word for such spaces is "companionway."

Nancy's son has converted a shed out back for those who want to hear good traditional music. To say the place is lively is an understatement. Anything can and does happen.

Tom Collins

Cecil Street

Owner Tess Collins, a regal, old-style "lady," is the hub of this superbly characterful pub, unchanged since the year dot except for the addition of a ladies' room. Lovely snug.

The Locke

On the Riverbank

The Locke is what is referred to as a "black and white pub"—a white façade with black trim. The pub, so named because of its location on the banks of the Shannon, is owned by the Costello family: Richard played rugby for Ireland. It's a rambling, meandering sort of place, long and narrow with lots of cubbies and crannies and a several open fires.

"Everyone" comes to The Locke—regular, local folk and legal eagles, rugby wags and students, hangers-on and punters. Says one habitué, "There's a fine average standard of behaviour maintained in here that everyone agrees to, a standard to which judges descend and vagabonds ascend."

Locke's is an especially good place to be in the summer time. Opposite the pub is a cobbled footpath along the river, a walkway lined with trees that are decorated with Japanese lanterns. In the evening, when the lanterns glow and the trees are in bloom, there's a kind of Parisian mood to it all that's very festive.

Music Tuesday and Wednesday.

Willie Sexton's

Henry Street

Owned by an ex-international rugby player, this pub has been recently and pleasantly modernised and features an open fire and good conversation.

South's

Top of O'Connell Street

This is a timeless old pub with a tranquillity akin to what you feel when looking at a painting of a Dutch interior. The floor is checkerboard black-and-white and the partitioned bar a cool white marble. When you sit down, its height is remarkable, reaching to chest level, and your glass is so close to your lips you barely need to raise it.

The wall behind the bar is a Victorian elaboration of curved mahogany arches framing bottles and antique painted mirrors. "John Jameson & Sons Old Malt" proclaims one mirror. Beneath the old-fashioned lettering are those hallmarks of Ireland: the greyhound, the harp, the castle, and the round tower.

To the side is a snug with walls of milk glass, and on the bulletin board in the rather more casual back room is a photographic roster of star rugby players. Behind this room is the back room, graced with a skylight and hunting tapestries.

I had heard that South's pours the best Guinness in town, and I can certainly recommend it. As I sat at the bar applying my own taste test to the brew, I gazed up at the coffered ceiling and tuned in on the conversation of two old men at a table behind me. It was all place names and family connections:

"John Daly was in yesterday. . ."

"John Daly? Now, would he be from Killarney?"

"No, that's Margaret O'Connor's boy you're tinkin' of."

"Margaret O'Connor? Her father came from Cork. . ." etc., etc.,

Note for the non-Irish reader: One of the most common questions a stranger is asked when entering a pub is "Where are ye from?" In Ireland this question is more than just curiosity. Here people identify closely with their home ground: they feel a bond with the corners of Ireland that "reared them up." Finding out where someone comes from is finding out who they are: each family name is associated with a specific region, i.e., O'Flannery with Limerick.

Listowel, Co. Kerry

Pronounced Lishtowel by Kerry people, this little town has become famous because of its special relationship with writers. Native sons: George Fitzmaurice, who wrote for the early Abbey Theatre; Maurice Walsh, author of *The Quiet Man*; Bryan McMahon (*Children of the Rainbow*); and, most visibly, John B. Keane, who combines two outstanding Irish gifts by being both a writer and publican.

John B., as he is affectionately referred to even by those who have never met him, is a prolific writer of books and plays. A controversial figure (some of the more snobbish literary types look down on him), he is beloved by many for his humour and his ability to depict the foibles and exact speech pattern of country folk with a compassionate irony that is, in itself, utterly Irish in character.

A thin, dark-haired man with a long face, John B. cares a great deal about writing, writers and the indigenous Irish culture and language. It is he who is responsible for loosing on Listowel a virtual blizzard of words in the form of Writers' Week.

Once a year, usually in July, the town of Listowel is utterly taken over by this event, in which swarms of writers and would-be scribes descend upon every available bed and breakfast, hotel, and pub to attend a giant series of conferences. There are poetry workshops and readings by the likes of Brendan Kennelly, Trinity College professor and poet. There are numerous awards, my favourite being the John Jameson Humorous Essay Open Competition. First prize in this competition is £150, plus a cut-glass decanter and a bottle of Jameson's whiskey (Joyce's favourite). This prize is considered appropriate for an Irish writer with wit.

There are musical events, plays, a book fair, an international poster exhibition, and of course, endless parties, both spontaneous and official. Inevitably, as in any Irish gathering, there is a great deal of talk, gossip, and conjecture, in this case most of it exceptionally sharp and epigrammatic.

John B. Keane's

> The world around us, particularly the rural world, is alive with singing language and fabulous characters, but there's little respect for the country poet anymore. . . . Every townland and parish is vibrant with the ballads of our departed poets. They're

waiting to be adopted and woven into the fabric of a living theatre, a theatre which is forcing its way upward and outward.

John B. Keane

The above, written by the owner of this pub, tells you a great deal about the flavour of his establishment. Physically, it is an intimate place with the conversational gap between bar and tables easily bridged. The room is small enough that the stranger might feel like an intruder upon entering, but don't be daunted—the natives are friendly after a brief interval.

I came to visit J.B.'s place on a day when the weather was what is euphemistically referred to in Kerry as "spiritual". A silvery drizzle dampened my hair as I walked along the streets discovering the nineteenth-century architectural delights peculiar to Listowel—stone sculptures over the doorways composed of lions, sunbursts, ladies, and birds.

In a wide street angling off to the left of Keane's, a horse fair was in progress. Ignoring the rain as all Irish country people do, a mingle of men of all ages lined the sides of the street. They watched with hooded interest as every now and again a horse, gleaming and slick with rain, was trotted past by his owner. Bargaining was so casual and low-key, so calm and conversational, it was hard to see it happen at all.

There were no writers here. They were all in workshops or pubs.

Note: the counter at J.B.K.'s has propped up the likes of Brian McMahon, Brendan Kennelly and John B. himself in regular combat for who can deliver the most astute observations on humanity.

The Horseshoe Bar

It's altogether too possible to spend more time than you had planned at the Horseshoe Bar. The pub is just *so* comfortable and it's such an interesting place to poke around in.

The building was erected in 1860 and the kitchen is made up of a series of small stables and storage spaces behind the restaurant—you can still see where the roofs connect to each other. Of course there have been renovations, but all has been done with the intention of keeping the pub as close to the original as possible. A case in point: when the floors were redone the flagstone was brought in from an old turn-of-the-century schoolhouse.

Irish theatre is a big theme at the Horseshoe, and the walls and ceilings are covered with posters and newspaper clippings of various productions. Among others you'll see the original poster for the 1945 production of Sean O'Casey's *Shadow Of A Gunman*, and the 1950 poster for *Sive*, a well-known play penned by Listowel's own native son, writer John B. Keane.

The Horseshoe also is the proud owner of two Jay Killian paintings. Jay, originally from Boston, has lived in Dingle for almost twenty years and is known for his paintings of bar scenes, and wonderful renditions of mood and atmosphere.

Over the bar is something that will make you look twice—a stuffed greyhound. He is Bearna Badghill who won the Tipperary Cup in February 1919 and is forever enshrined for his effort. Bearna was over the bar in 1940 when Liam Wolfe took over the pub and the present proprietor, his son Kevin, has no intention of removing him. "Bearna's part of the pub's history," Kevin says.

Kevin can be found everywhere, cooking in the kitchen, tending the bar, seating people in the upstairs restaurant (seats about 40), making cappuccino, sweeping the floor. With his sense of untiring commitment to excellence it's no wonder the pub won the 1988 Kerry Pub of the Year Award.

Traditional music every Sunday night.

The Maid of Erin

A nicely refurbished little pub with an interesting display of the work and life of the local the local stonemason and architect Pat McAuliffe. Most of the distinctive plaster and stone works in Listowel are his creations.

The Thatch

A "new" thatched roof pub built from the ground up, with a rustic feel and the glow of gas lamps. A live ceili band every night as well as ceili dancing.

Midleton, Co. Cork

Back in the mists of time the Irish called it "Uisce Beatha," the "Water of Life." Now, visitors can trace the history of the magical spirit at Jameson Heritage Centre at Midleton.

In 1966, the whiskey houses of Ireland joined together to become the Irish Distiller's Group. Following this merger, the

Group built a new distilling complex alongside the Old Midleton Distillery, which had been producing fine whiskey for 150 years.

Instead of abandoning the beautiful buildings and distilling machinery of a bygone era, the Group have turned the Old Distillery into a learning centre where the visitor can spend an hour being entertained and educated about the world of "spirits."

The walking tour begins at the courtyard where farmers brought their barley. Next come the kilns where the barley was dried and germinated, after which you can see the 150-year-old water wheel, and the machinery and vats where the whiskey-making process continued on its merry way. Appropriately, the tour ends with a stop at the cooperage where the casks were made, and is completed at the "Jameson Bar" with a "taste" of, what else, Irish whiskey. I don't know whether it was because of all that walking and learning, but by the time we got to the "bar" part, I had built up a powerful thirst, and the whiskey tasted extra good.

For those who would like less spirited refreshment, there's a coffee shop on the premises.

Miltown Malbay, Co. Clare

I arrived in Miltown Malbay under the worst and the best possible circumstances. It was pouring rain and it was the week in July when this little town becomes a centre for all truly devoted practitioners of Irish traditional music, with emphasis on piping.

My companions were three young Dubliners who brought with them a wide assortment of jokes, a guitar and a set of Uilleann pipes. We parked at the end of a line of cars that stretched ever farther out of town as new devotees continued to arrive.

Actually, in July, the entire county of Clare becomes one giant music festival. A few miles up the coast, Lisdoonvarna was hosting 20,000 fans, but friends had assured me that "the real craic" was here in Miltown Malbay. They must have been right. I saw a member of The Chieftains band in a local restaurant. He must have sneaked away from the action for a secret hour here among the "cognoscenti."

This little town is the birthplace of the great piper Willy Clancy, and the festival is a kind of fraternity party for pipers from all over the world. Aside from (literally) non-stop music and talk, there are workshops where you can learn not only how to play but how to *make* pipes.

And where is the music played? Yes, of course, in pubs. The musicians move from one pub to another all afternoon and deep into the night, switching venues for fresh inspiration and partners. The visitor to Miltown Malbay will do best to follow their example.

As I made the rounds of the pubs with my friends, time stopped and the experience became a melange of music and pints shot through with talk and laughter.

The musicians are a bizarre mix of nationalities and types: "auld fellas" whose skills are legendary, yet who make music as naturally as they plant fields; wild-haired youngsters with intense faces who grow tired and drunk and fall asleep under the tables and on the benches; woolly-sweatered girls in long skirts; straight-laced intellectuals; shambling students wearing American University T-shirts; ordinary people from the Irish countryside. Some of these are magicians who can play you into a trance, others are there to learn.

The pubs are full of people from miles around: families, children and local people clap, sing and celebrate.

Officially the pubs close at 11.30 p.m. What this means is that the doors are locked at 11.30 p.m. No one may enter and those who leave are not permitted back in. Behind the locked doors a mood of intimacy sets in; the publican brings out refreshments, and the true musicians hit their stride. It is wise therefore, to make a quick tour of the pubs before 11.30 to make sure you'll be in the right spot to hear the best music when the clock strikes closing time.

The unlucky ones who are left standing outside try every means to get in. They crowd around the locked doors knocking and when the barman opens up a crack, they employ every device known to the inventive Irish mind to weave stories that will allow them in. The beleaguered barman rewards one or two with the best stories by letting them slip through the conspiratorially half-open door.

One of my companions was caught outside at 11.30 and told the publican that he absolutely had to gain entry because his girlfriend was inside and he felt an intense urge to propose marriage to her at that very instant. He didn't make it, though his story provided a good laugh for the crowd inside.

Finally, at 3.00 a.m., the publican closed up shop, but the musicians kept going until dawn.

When we came out of our pub, a thin moon shone on the squat stone houses. The crowd milled around under the streetlight in front of the pub; then a tin whistle took up a reel, the notes clear and flowing as an upland stream. People crowded around the player, and upstairs the publican's children, who had just finished collecting glasses for their father, leaned out to listen. "That's Mary Bergen playing," whispered my Dublin friend; "she's the best in the land." After a bewitching few moments, Mary was joined by a guitar and fiddle, and as I walked away, people old and young had begun to dance, illuminated by the pale moon and the circle of light from the street lamp.

A minute later I was in the total darkness of the sweet-smelling Irish night, driving through fields towards the sea.

A word of caution: You must either be prepared to not sleep at all, to sleep in your car, or to make reservations well in advance for lodging during this festival.

Three good Miltown Malbay pubs are MICHAEL A'S, MICKY WILSON'S and PAT HENNESSY'S.

SCHULL, CO. CORK

A few miles from Ballydehob is Schull, another artists' centre and favourite port of call for international yachtsmen.

Schull is a small fishing village sheltered from the north winds by Mt Gabriel. From the harbour you can see the group of islands known as the Carbery's Hundred Islands. Take the ferry for an afternoon on Cape Clear Island, a windswept, green-carpeted, flower-strewn rock where life is old and custom timeless. On the way you will see the solitary Fastnet Rock lighthouse, Ireland's most southern point.

So much for geography. Actually, what separates Schull from its sister villages in West Cork is not the savagery of its name or its unexpected cuteness and go-lightly grace, nor even its cosmopolitanism. What makes Schull different is the resonant fact that it produces, sells and serves some of the finest food to be found in Ireland.

To take just one example among the products of the farmers, gardeners, bakers and cake-makers, the village is bracketed by two extraordinary cheese makers — Bill Hogan to the east and Giana Ferguson to the west. Bill's fabulous cheeses, Gabriel, Desmond and Mizen, are inspired by the hard style Gruyère types, while Giana's equally memorable Gubbeen Farmhouse cheese is akin to the creamy Pont L'Évêque.

The quality of the fish goes without saying.

THE BLACK SHEEP INN

Main Street

This is a truly quaint, rambling old inn with a charming entrance through an alleyway. The back garden is a green and flowery retreat and the bar food and restaurant are famous both locally and as far away as Dublin. The pub features spontaneous and organised music and is comfortably furnished.

Overheard at The Black Sheep Inn: "There's a lot of truth to the lies you tell."

THE BUNRATTY INN

The Bunratty Inn, up on top of the hill, was once such a desperate dive and famous fleapit that the owners mischievously named it after what was then the most famous, celebrated and expensive hostelry in the country. It is no longer a dive, having become a professional and pristine pub, but it's still The Bunratty and the droll sense of humour abides.

The home-made salmon salad and brown bread are particularly scrumptious here, but all the food is not only delicious but very good value. You can test the truth of this claim either at the bar, in the back room, or in summer, on a nice little porch.

NEWMAN'S CORNER HOUSE

Main Street

Newman's *is* on the corner. It is a grocery shop-pub and a centre for local news, as well as a good spot for a spontaneous musical interlude. Yachtsmen and fishermen all gravitate to Newman's laid-back, seen-it-all-before atmosphere where impish humour is the order of the day and the subjects for conversation are equally divided between fish and regattas, both of which abound here in West Cork.

The pub is presided over by Kitty Newman (it's been in her family for 70 years).

Newman's is the place where you apply for your permit to fish the reservoir for the rainbow trout stocked there. This pub is always lively, but it is particularly amusing during Schull Festival Week (usually sometime in mid July). My favourite event of the festival, apart from the singing competition, is the pub-to-pub wheelbarrow race.

Some Notes On The West Cork Area

In this area Ireland outdoes herself in treats for the visitor: you can easily rent boats, go deep-sea fishing or diving (see the harbour master in Schull), go pony trekking (Schull or Bantry), rent bikes (Schull), play tennis (courts outside Schull) or golf (Bantry or Skibbereen).

Day trips and walks could keep you in the area for weeks. Glengarriff, while quite overrun with tourists, is a must. A little village on the Beara peninsula, it snuggles in a mythically fertile glen. The valley, though rocky, is thickly wooded with oaks, elms, pines, yew, and holly, as well as various Mediterranean-type plants flowering their hearts out. Visit Garinish Island there and the exceptional gardens open to the public. Glengarriff will make a poet out of you. Even if you can't write it down, the ancient spell woven of water, air, light, and foliage will never be forgotten. (For a pleasing Glengarrif pub, try The Blue Loo on Main Street).

If you are driving on a Sunday in West Cork, be careful. Just around the next bend you might encounter the favourite pastime of road bowling. A 28-ounce (800 g) cast-iron ball is lofted across a curve and flung along a measured course on the road, drawing an excited Sunday crowd of betters.

SNEEM, CO. KERRY

THE BLUE BULL

Sneem is so very small that if you blink when you're passing through you'll be out of town already, but it has five good pubs. I particularly like The Blue Bull, owned by the Carroll family. It's a clean, traditional style pub with good food and good Guinness, popular with cosmopolitans and locals alike. Keep an eye out for the ex-postman whose cow calves fifty-two times a year.

For a particularly beautiful drive, take the back road from Kilorglan to Sneem through Ballaghbeana and Ballagoisin. Don't miss the lush gardens of Sneem's Parknasilla Hotel.

TEMPLEMORE, CO. TIPPERARY

POLLY'S PUB

Prizewinning, intimate pub with good food, "caring" staff and "doll's house" décor, at the gates of the Garda College.

Terryglass, Co. Tipperary

Paddy's Pub

If you love to fish or just take a leisurely ride on a lake cruiser, stop off at this pub on the shores of Lough Derg. This one was recommended to me by the writer and wit, Hugh Leonard, who says: "You can almost spot Paddy's Pub in Terryglass from the bridge of your cruiser as you approach the tiny harbour in the Northeast corner of Lough Derg; it is a short walk up a winding lane, and you are no sooner in this tiny hamlet than you are out of it. But the pub is small, dark and a jewel of its kind." (See Dromineer for Leonard's other Lough Derg recommendation, about 90 minutes cruising time away).

Thurles, Co. Tipperary

Frances Glasheen, Holycross

Quiet, dark pub in beautiful setting adjoining a fourteenth century abbey still in use.

O'Gorman's

Superb pub in the family for generations. Pot-bellied stove in the middle of a stone floored bar. Legendary Tuesday night sessions, often with up to 20 musicians. Back yard has famine cottages in varying degrees of decay.

Tipperary, Co. Tipperary

Corny's

Fantastic ancient pub peopled by all types of humanity. Lovely fire, magic ambience that just oozes atmosphere. Unleavable.

Tidge Malone's

Davis Street

A purely, utterly plain Irish small-town pub—no snugs, no antiques, but a whole wall of postcards, some yellowed with age, some scenic, some ribald, some unusual.

I was taken there by an old pony trekking guide who had befriended me. At first we had a bit of a hard time understanding each other, between my American accent and his toothless and very thick brogue, but somewhere during the evening, laughter completely vanquished the language barrier.

It's by no means a sure thing that Tidge's will be open—sometimes he keeps his door closed to all, even though you know "the knock" to get in. As my friend said, "there's a knock to gettin' in, but I can tell you too, once you're in, there's a knack to gettin out."

TRALEE, CO. KERRY

She was lovely and fair
As the rose of the summer
But t'was not her beauty alone
That won me.
Ah no, t'was the love in her eyes
Forever a'dawnin'
That made me love Mary
The Rose of Tralee.

William Mulchinock

The capital of Kerry, gateway to the Dingle Peninsula, Tralee is a Georgian town of 13,000 souls known for its pleasant beaches and the Rose of Tralee Festival in August. At this time, amid much drinking and singing of ballads, the Rose is chosen. She and her court of beautiful runner-ups are then escorted to a ball by the most eligible of the young bachelors of Kerry—to dance the night away in the best of Kerry society.

If you fancy roses of the floral variety, you'll find a charming rose garden and a small memorial in the town park dedicated to William Mulchinock, the composer of the famous and much sentimentalised ballad "The Rose of Tralee."

BAILY'S CORNER

Dickensian style pub with magnetism for everyone, owned by a charismatic, travelled wit and master of engaging discourse.

GLENDUFF HOUSE

Keilduff

Family-run bar-restaurant and country home in rural, rustic surroundings. Converted eighteenth-century manor with chalets where the stables once were.

Lynche's of the Spa

5 miles (8 km) out of Tralee on the Fenit road

In this pub there is almost always someone sitting at the piano, singing. The bar is extra-long and the seafood the best in the area.

For history buffs: St Brendan the Navigator, credited in some circles with the discovery of America, was born in this neighbourhood.

Waterford, Co. Waterford

Beautifully situated on the River Suir, Waterford is one of Ireland's leading ports and harbours an enormous amount of container traffic to the south of England and to the Continent. So it comes as no surprise to learn that Waterford is a commercial city. What is surprising is the nature of one of Waterford's largest businesses—education.

As a town of many schools, both day and boarding, Waterford's streets are filled with an unusually large percentage of young faces, their freshness forming an interesting contrast to the ancient walls, crumbling ruins, and storied past of this city.

It was in the eighteenth century that the city began to truly enjoy economic prosperity and from 1783 to 1851 produced the marvellous heavy glass that was to make Waterford's name famous around the world. Then, in 1851, as a result of the Great Famine and the ensuing depression that swept Ireland, the glassworks closed; for a century no one made so much as a drinking glass in Waterford.

In 1952, a new factory was opened and hand-blown and engraved Waterford is again pleasing the world market. On average, the Waterford master blowers and engravers are probably the youngest in the world, having been apprenticed in their craft at the age of fifteen. This happy state of affairs has meant that Waterford men no longer need to emigrate to seek their fortunes but can prosper at home.

Glass is for sale at Knox's and at Palmer's in Waterford, and a great example of old Waterford crystal is on display in the Chamber of the Public Library Building in the form of a magical chandelier.

The Auld Stand
John Street
A corner pub done in the classic London style, with good bar food and a restaurant upstairs.

T.& H. Doolin
George Street
Doolin's is just off the pedestrian mall where you can pleasure your eye with some nicely restored eighteenth century buildings. You'll think you're in a country bar here in this intimate pub. Two rooms side by side, dimly lit and timbered. A friendly crowd. Good folk sessions.

Jordan's American Bar
The Quay
Take a walk along the Quay past the famous Reginald's Tower and the amusing shops until you reach this docker's pub that has beautifully withstood the test of time and the winds of fashion.

The tiny bar is most unusual. Appropriately, considering its harbour-side location, it feels rather like the snug cabin of a boat. The eighteenth century wood wall trim, inset drawers and clock are in ship-shape condition, as is the little wooden guard rail around the edges of the somewhat high bar.

The entrance door has a picture of an American eagle holding a flag and inside, all along the top moulding of the wall, is a collection of old American car licence plates. No one seemed to know why, however.

Dart games some evenings.

Youghal, Co. Cork

Youghal is thirty miles (48 km) from the city of Cork. It has several claims to fame besides its expansive beach: it is known for its point lace or "pointe d'Irlande," a lace with a vivid pattern; as well as Myrtle Grove, the stately Elizabethan building that was once Sir Walter Raleigh's home. According to tradition, Raleigh smoked the first tobacco to come to Ireland from the New World. As he sat puffing a pipe under a yew tree at Myrtle Grove, a servant, alarmed at the smoke, threw a bucket of water over his master to extinguish the fire. And it was in the garden at Myrtle Grove that Sir Walter is said to have grown the first spuds, plants brought from America.

Aherne's Seafood Bar

North Main Street

Family-run (third generation) this spotless, nautical pub is literally a prizewinner, having repeatedly won Ireland's National Bar Food competition. The seafood *is* delicious—any fresher and it would be swimming. You can enjoy your food at the bar or go to the restaurant in the back.

An added enticement: if you get too "happy" to drive you can stay overnight. Aherne's ten rooms could be said to have some of the biggest beds in Ireland: "Could sleep an entire band," as a friend put it.

Guests are truly made to feel welcome, and the staff's effort to be friendly and to "get it right" adds to the qualities which make Aherne's a very special spot.

CONNACHT

Athleague, Co. Roscommon

Fitzmaurice's Tavern

The owner of this tavern, Roger Dobson, has managed to create a pub that combines the best aspects of a bar and a museum. There's an absolute wealth of objects here, many of them agricultural, almost all of them worthy conversation pieces. The service is cheerful, the open fire is cosy and the food is good home-made fare—soup, sandwiches, chicken, ham—all cooked by Angela Dobson herself.

Ballisodare, Co. Sligo

Beach Bar

At the junction of N4 and N59 at Ballisodore, take the N59 for Ballina. On the way, you'll find a sparklingly pristine, whitewashed pub with a thatched roof and eye popping views of Aughris Bay.

The Beach Bar is where the old and the new meet—literally. The senior local people gather in the "old" front room (the most "venerable" part of the building is 300 years old, but was wallpapered sometime in the 50s) and the more "contemporary" crowd gravitate towards the modern extension. (I rather like drifting back and forth between the two—it's like stereo versus mono transmission).

The proprietors are Peter and Maura McDermott. Peter was born in Augher's Bay, a very rare thing indeed. The village at one time had twenty two families, but now only Mrs Winnie Martin, who returned home from the United States, lives there. According to Matty Golden, a local historian, the population began dropping when the cove stopped being used for smuggling.

None of this affects business at the Beach Bar, which is thriving, especially on weekends and in the summertime.

During the warm months, Bay camping is available, and B&B rooms can be booked year round.

The Beach Bar serves chicken, salmon, burgers, steak and kidney pie, chips and chowders. Traditional music or country western on weekends.

The Thatch

Established 1638, originally a coaching Inn in the seventeenth and eighteenth centuries. Stand outside the Thatch for a few moments just to admire this three hundred year old building which has survived the added comforts and cleanliness of modernisation without losing an iota of charm. The thatched roof is flawless, the doorways and eaves are draped in vines, a story-book effect, and the thick cottage walls are so white they are almost blinding.

The interior lives up to the promise of the exterior. Walls mellowed with the smoke of turf fires are covered with interesting photographs of Irish life at the turn of the century. Three snug-like enclosures to the right of the bar cosily accommodate ten to twelve people.

A back room area with two fireplaces, a much larger bar, and tables and chairs is equally inviting.

Brian Fizpatrick is the proprietor and the Thatch has been in his family since 1828. He's a delightful host with a winning smile and infectious laugh. Ask to see the garden even if the weather isn't appropriate for outside pleasures. It's a beauty.

Traditional music and song, soup and sandwiches and the occasional special.

Ballycroy, Co. Mayo

Cleary's

On the N59 road from Bangor to Mullrany

The road from Bangor to Mulrany twists and turns, taking you through some of Ireland's most hauntingly barren countryside. There is only one town along its entire length, Ballycroy. Actually, Ballycroy should be renamed Cleary's, since this pub-grocer's/social centre/post office *is* the town. There's even a phone booth outside. "Provisions Store," it says in the window, and the sign says, "CLEARY'S, BAR GROCERY."

Cleary's has been the domain of the Cleary family for over 150 years and is the centre of all the neighbouring activities. If you visit on a Sunday, you'll meet the entire population of Ballycroy at Cleary's—that is if you visit after mass—the church is just behind the pub. After mass, the men gather in one of the two bars and the women in the other. The kids flock to the large well stocked grocery store section looking at magazines, drinking soft drinks and, of course, buying sweets.

Phyllis and Louis Cleary were married in 1939 and since Louis passed away Phyllis has been running Cleary's herself. She's an active and spirited "young" lady with a memory that a Rhodes scholar would envy. She has a passion for gardening which she indulges in a small and beautiful plot to the rear of the house by the kitchen. It's a sweet spot with a fountain at its heart and a small army of cats as its protectors.

Genealogical note: Phyllis is a first cousin of Eileen O'Casey (Sean O'Casey's widow) and has the family good looks.

BALLYHAUNIS, CO. MAYO

VAL'S BAR

Here's a Mayo pub with the imprimatur of an Irish writer, in this case Hugh Leonard. "I've had the great good fortune to be a judge in the finals of the "Top Pub" contest for several years, which probably provided the groundwork for a well-earned Ph.D., Pub Hunting Diploma," he remarks.

His comment on Val's: "Halfway up a muddy street, this is an oasis in the desert of east Mayo. The bar is small, warm, bright and welcoming; there is usually a turf fire burning and the pub grub is excellent. I have travelled miles out of my way across the flat, wet bogland, just to call on Val's and bask in the friendliness."

BARNA, CO. GALWAY

DONNELLEY'S OF BARNA

This pub was originally a thatched cottage before it was renovated and extended at the turn of the century to become a pub-grocery. The same family still run it, and do a very nice job too. They've modernised with an eye towards keeping a low ceilinged "cottagey" feel without sacrificing comfort. Aside from the delicious seafood specialities, this bar offers steaks, chicken dishes and one or two vegetarian dishes such as mushroom and vegetable Stroganoff.

In the back where the stables used to be, is a restaurant attractively decorated along nautical lines. I couldn't help but imagine how surprised the former tenants would be if they could see people having a leisurely evening meal where once the horses munched their grain.

BOYLE, CO. ROSCOMMON

Roscommon is an inland county where the main attraction is the beauty of the many island-dotted lakes that drowse in the countryside of level plains, bogland, river meadow, and low hills. Roscommon and Boyle are the county's main towns.

Two miles northeast of Boyle in the Rockingham demesne is Lough Key Forest Park, a good place for a walk and a picnic. On an island in the lake are the ruins of the Abbey of Trinity. Here medieval monks once compiled a local history, and in the shadow of its walls are the graves of Tomás Costello and Una MacDermot, an Irish Romeo and Juliet. After Una died, Tomás wrote for her one of the most beautiful love songs in any language: "Oh, fair Una, like a rose in a garden you,/ And like a candlestick of gold you were on/ The table of a queen. . . ."

On the north side of the town of Boyle are the ruins of Boyle Abbey, Connacht's most important medieval abbey.

Midway between Carrick and Boyle is Cootehall, where the writer John McGahern grew up. His early novels deal with the realities of life in the west with a hard yet tender honesty. He is a master at evoking the rain-soaked and lonely landscape of Roscommon and the intricacies of parent-child relationships. McGahern presently lives in Foxfield, near Carrick-on-Shannon, just across the border in Leitrim.

The Four Provinces

On the Boyle-Croghan road

This pub, out in the middle of nowhere about five miles (8 km) from Boyle, attracts large numbers of people from miles around. It is a real country pub, with a small bar, a stage for musicians, and a back room that is opened up for nights when there is dancing. Live music four nights a week.

Carrick-on-Shannon, Co. Leitrim

Flyn's

This little old pub sits beside the second smallest church in all of Ireland. The pub is furnished with tables that were once meant for sewing machines and seats that formerly were pews. Flyn's is a real "pint bar"—small, cosy, and cute.

Clarinbridge, Co. Galway

Paddy Burke's Oyster Inn

Paddy Burke's is one of Ireland's most renowned pubs and restaurants. It is a snug thatched pub genuinely traditional in atmosphere. The low ceiling is beamed, and there are high-backed benches and rope-seat stools. Small leaded windowpanes let in a soft light, and a large fieldstone fireplace reminds you of Ireland's reputation for hospitality. On the wall is an unusual painting of Blind Raftery the poet. His smile is oddly insinuating, in disconcerting contrast to his vacant eyes.

At the impeccably polished three-sided bar local people, visiting Dubliners, and tourists congregate. "Cars park themselves here automatically, you know," a Dublin man told me; "they're that used to making the stop. This area is called the Bermuda Triangle," he went on. "Between Paddy Burke's, Moran's the Weir, and the Kilkeene Graveyard, people have been known to completely disappear."

Clarinbridge is an oyster town, and in season (September-April) Paddy's serves these mouth-watering morsels fresh. There's also a splendid variety of buffet foods to satisfy the most gourmet palate, and a Cordon Bleu menu at night (prices are fairly reasonable).

With all these delights, it is no wonder that this pub, in operation since 1835, should have been discovered and frequented by the famous and infamous. Royalty, both British and the Hollywood type, have made Paddy's a favourite port of call in Ireland, as have men and women prominent in international news.

Raftery the Poet

I am Raftery the poet
Full of hope and love,
With eyes without light
And calm without torment.

Going west on my journey
By the light of my heart,
Weak and tired
To my road's end.

Look at me now,
My face to the wall,
Playing music
To empty pockets.

Anthony Raftery
(translated from the Irish by
Frank O'Connor)

Clifden, Co. Galway

The main town of Connemara, Clifden is a good centre from which to explore the area. Connemara seems to swallow people; no matter how many tourists flock there, the solitude is vast and healing. From Clifden you can strike out on a variety of inland or coastal rambles and return refreshed.

The town proper is two broad streets of brightly painted shops and a marketplace that in August is the site of the Connemara Pony Fair, honouring this hardy Irish horse. Breeders from all over the world rub shoulders with the locals, the tinkers, and the three-card tricksters.

There are two excellent shops in Clifden: Millar's which produces handwoven tweeds in glowing colours, and Stanley's—a real country store with a jumble of everything you could imagine, from fishing rods to high fashion to mattress ticking. There are also craft shops stocking the famous Connemara marble (visit the quarry at nearby Streamstown), Galway crystal, and tweeds.

The Connemara Golf Course, about ten miles (16 km) south of Clifden, is so beautifully situated it's hard to keep your eye on the ball; stretches of fine, sandy beaches run beside it, and the Twelve Bens supervise your game from the distance (Ben means mountain).

E. J. King's

In 1992 owner Terry Sweeney renovated this lively, old bar situated in the town square. But fear not—Terry's modernisation didn't alter the pub's basic cosy atmosphere. Instead, the addition of an airy atrium and bright colours on the upper floors only add to this pub's traditional pleasures. The menu includes lovely seafood as a matter of course, and blackboard "specials" typically feature such goodies as bacon and cabbage, roast beef or rack of lamb and a good choice of farmhouse cheeses.

Live music nightly in season, two or three nights during the winter. Mainly folk and ballads.

Collooney, Co. Sligo

Johnnie Mac's

Between Sligo and Castlebaldwin on the Dublin Road (N4) is Johnnie Mac's, a pub stop for the past two centuries.

Like most old pubs in Ireland, the front room once was a grocery store. Today, both front and back rooms are in "pub" use, and the traveller looking for a pleasant stop will find a welcoming fire and good "chat." When the weather is right, there's a pretty garden out back for indulging in the outdoor pint, and even if the weather is "soft," (translation for the non Irish reader "mizzle") there's a tarpaulin for the outdoorsy drinker to shelter under.

The pub's friendly owners, Mary and Andy Spring, live upstairs.

Dromahair, Co. Leitrim

This is Yeats country, at the south end of Lough Gill. Dromahair is a quiet village and if your name is O'Rourke, you'll be interested to know that this area is the family's ancestral land and they were once a mighty clan here.

STANFORD'S VILLAGE INN

The McGowan family, who own Stanford's, have ample experience in the fine art of "publicanism"—they've been running this one for five generations. The tavern has been recently renovated, but fortunately for us all, it remains "the real thing," a good, simple place to meet friends and enjoy a "jar."

There are several comfortable bars with fires where you can choose from a bar menu of plain but very good salads, soups, and sandwiches. Should you want to get more complicated, gustatorially speaking, Stanford's also has a restaurant.

DRUMCLIFFE, CO. SLIGO

The magnificent twenty two miles from Sligo to Bundoran are high above the bay of Drumcliffe, passing the access road to Drumcliffe churchyard, where W.B. Yeats lies buried. This road is marked, somehow appropriately, by an ancient Celtic cross and the remains of a round tower. Rooks gather in the old trees around the church, and in among the grasses and gravestones is a plain slab of limestone carrying the message written by Yeats himself as his epitaph:

Cast a cold eye
On life, on death.
Horseman, pass by!

Of course, with lovely Irish irony, no one simply passes by. Horsemen and travellers using more modern means of transport linger and cast anything but a cold eye. Fortunately, however, there are no great tourist hordes or buses, just a few people wandering about in the peaceful shade. Sometimes an admirer will lay a fresh flower upon the grave, where it glows against the gravel covering.

Though Yeats died in Paris, he requested burial in Sligo, picking this particular churchyard because his great-grandfather had once been rector there.

Drumcliffe is flanked by the extraordinary, flat-topped landmark of Benbulben Mountain on one side and Knocknarea Mountain on the other. Knocknarea is traditionally considered to be the tomb of Maeve, the first century A.D. Queen of Connacht. On the summit is the great cairn within which it is said she lies, a mound of stones with a slope 80 feet (24.4 m) high, a diameter 100 feet (30.5 m) at the top and 630 feet (192 m) around the bottom. A number of satellite tombs surround the cairn, keeping Maeve company in death. This warrior queen of the ancient sagas is another female personification of Ireland, another manifestation of the Irish fertility goddess.

The Yeats Tavern

This large, award winning pub in the "new" traditional style is the place to stop after you've soaked up all that Yeatsiana. If it's a bit of grub you want along with your drink there are daily specials such as Irish stew, or Dublin Coddle along with the usual bar menu. Try the garden, weather permitting, it's a refreshing one.

> The bane of small-town publican's life is the loudmouthed loquacious customer who, keeping his drink in front of him for hours on end, warrants his presence in the bar by sips taken at fifteen minute intervals. The publican's admonition to such may well be the brutal but effective "Come on, pelt it down ye!" but I admire the approach of the spruce old widow, who, gazing over the rim of her glasses, rebuked the vehement with "Gentlemen, I'm afraid your conversation is curtailing your capacity."
>
> *Danny Costello,*
> *"The Small-Town Pub"*

Galway City

Galway is billed as the "Gateway to the West, " and so it is—a funnel through which you pass to the enormous solitude of Connemara and the heart of the western Gaeltacht.

The city of Galway is wedged between the sea and the great expanse of Lough Corrib, which stretches deep into the land of the west, covering sixty-eight square miles (21 sq km) of some of the best fishing in the world. It is said to have an island for each day of the year. These islands vary in size, from verdant acres to tiny bird sanctuaries. One island is approached at your own risk—it is patrolled by a mad one-horned goat.

At Galway the Lough empties out into the River Corrib, out to sea and into Galway Bay. If you're in the city during the months of December, January or February, stand on the Weir Bridge spanning the river and look down. You'll see the annual miracle of thousands of salmon lying on the river bed. They are waiting for the rain to raise the water level so that they can leap upstream to their spawning grounds in the lakes and rivers.

In summer (July) the city hosts the annual Galway Film Festival, a gala event which draws film folk from around the world, both the serious and the glitzy.

If you're in town some time around 17 August, you'll be there in time for the races. Ask any old-timer about the Galway races and you'll get a knowing wink. "Ah, they'll be lying in the fields and everywhere that week," said one old gent to me. "Well," he sighed, "but it's not what it used to be."

From what I hear it's still a great auld celebration, with oceans of Guinness and much laughter and music. As for what it used to be . . . you know, I think lying in the fields isn't all that bad.

Galway Arms

Lower Dominick Street

At the head of Lower Dominick Street stands a large, two-storey Tudor type building, almost out of place in the context of its more prosaic surroundings. This is the Galway Arms, established 1828 and survivor of several metamorphoses. Originally two pubs married together at the turn of the century, the inside is spacious with several fireplaces and quite a few interesting artifacts. The pub lunch is good and at noon the place is jammed with a melange of tourists and local business people. The upstairs serves as a function hall.

The Great Southern Hotel/O'Flaherty's

15 Eyre Square

The renowned Great Southern Hotel was once called the Railroad Hotel. Erected in 1845 in the heyday of the great locomotives, it still exudes an atmosphere of old-world values, of reliability, solid comfort and elegance.

The hotel's pub, O'Flaherty's, was originally the wine cellar, and several of the cellar's supporting arches, (circa 1840) lead into snugs fittingly filled with railroad memorabilia: photos and drawings of locomotives with names like The Giant, The Chieftain, and The Dubliner, and even an 1886 map showing the routes and destinations of the Midland Great Western Railway.

Carvery lunch, good traditional menu. Entertainment and dance floor on weekends.

O'Flaherty's can be entered from the hotel lobby or from the street.

McAlinden's

Lower Dominick Street

The sign outside says established 1893, but as with many pubs in Ireland, McAlinden's has been modernised—very tastefully so in this case. The seventy foot (21 m) bar (long, even for Ireland) is polished mahogany and the comfortable banquette seating opposite the bar is upholstered in a mute mauve. Stained glass windows and a cosy snug in the rear complete the picture.

Gerrard and Marie McAlinden own the pub and they have a great sense of humour. Near the cash register there are two signs: one says "no singing" and the other is a musical note with an x through it.

If you've exhausted yourself with a bout of shopping at the tempting stores on lower Dominick Street, McAlinden's is a convenient place to recover.

McSwiggan's

3 Eyre Street

In 1986, Tom and Stephanie Smyth took over a small pub called Paddy O'Flynn's and, like fairy god-parents, transformed it into an outstanding dining, drinking and entertainment emporium. And the word emporium might be a bit of an understatement. McSwiggin's has three levels, four bars, six dining areas — one marvels at the design and fluidity of the place.

Here you can go for a pub crawl without leaving the premises. You can start at the ground floor where Paddy's small pub is still the warm heart of the establishment, or the Film Room where autographed photos of movie stars gaze down at you. Or rise above it all in the Courtyard Bar where you can see all the levels of McSwiggin's. In the Courtyard, a rowing scull is suspended above the heads of the revellers, the gift of the prize-winning Galway Rowing Club, sponsored by the Smyths.

There's a good carvery, the menu is varied, well prepared and well served.

If you have time, ask Tom about the history of the building, it's fascinating.

O'CONNELL'S

Eyre Square

If you are an aficionado of single malt scotch, O'Connell's is your pub. Here you'll find one of the best selections in Ireland and a publican, Dave Lonegra, who likes nothing more than to discuss the distinguishing marks and merits of the various choices.

Dave and Annette bought the pub seven years ago from the O'Connell family, who had owned the bar from the turn of the century.

Originally a grocery store and small bar (the etched glass door still proclaims it to be a "Grocery and Bar") it was converted to a full bar about twenty years ago. A new counter top was put in, but everything else is just as it has been since 1929. You'll find a vintage pressed tin ceiling, a tiled floor and tiles behind the bar. (Take note of the little blue tiles behind the bar, they should be preserved by order of the National Trust).

The stained glass windows and the overhead lighting are all original and in mint condition and the fox over the window is claimed to have been in situ since 1910.

Worthy of special attention: a framed photo on the wall entitled "The Old Claddagh Scene" (a forceful yet tender depiction of life in Ireland 100 years ago), and a classified page from the "Police Gazette Hue-and-Cry" of 9 June 1874 listing the advertisements of people trying to locate relatives.

O'Connell's is a genuine local pub—no music or food, but good atmosphere, congenial customers, and then of course there's Dave and the single malts.

Entertainment changes nightly, and it's wise to book reservations: 091 68917.

O'CONNOR'S

Situated on Galway Bay just outside Galway City, O'Connor's was established in 1854. The present owners, Cornelius and son Tom, are the third generation of O'Connors to run this very popular pub famous for seafood and music. It's a "singing pub," which is to say that if you enjoy a good sing-song you'll love it.

O'Connor's is packed floor to ceiling with an amazing array of artifacts and if you went there every night for a week, more than likely you still wouldn't see all the objects clinging to the walls, squeezed in the corners and hanging from the ceiling. The mood is one of true gaiety, fun and laughter. An eye popping extravaganza.

THE SNUG-GARAVAN'S

Shop Street

The Snug-Garavan's is a study in positive schizophrenia. It's actually two pubs in one, yet each has its own very distinct and separate character.

Upon entering The Snug you get the feeling of being in an ancient cellar, which in fact you are. At the rear of the pub is an alcove which was originally a large hearth. The beam above the hearth has been dated through dendrochronology (a method of dating wood) to approximately 1292. Although the alcove now contains tables and chairs, the warm aura of ancient fires still seems to linger in the air.

The stone walls and ceilings are whitewashed and the decorations, mostly photographs, lithographs and artifacts relevant to the Galway, are a delightfully painless way to learn the city's history.

The upper portion of the two buildings dates from the sixteenth and seventeenth century. Renovations are under way, and if architecture is one of your pleasures, you'll be interested in the second floor fireplace and the daub and wattle walls (made with hazel wood branches and plaster).

Garavan's, like a fraternal twin, is completely different. It's open, woody and decorated in a more "traditional" pub fashion. (Until two years ago it still contained a grocery store which has since been replaced by "the Yeltsin Lounge," so named because rumour has it that the famous Russian indulged in some Galway Vodka here one evening).

Both pubs serve a pub menu. Traditional music Thursdays and Sundays. Jazz and Blues, Fridays and Saturdays.

TIGH NEACHTAIN/NAUGHTON'S

17 Cross Street

If this "pub of character" could talk it would surely tell some fascinating tales. The building was once the townhouse of Richard Martin M.P., founder of the Royal Society for the Prevention of Cruelty to Animals (nicknamed "Humanity Dick" by George IV). It is one of the last buildings still standing in Galway city that dates back to medieval times and is also one of the few buildings with a genuine, intact oriel window. The interior, I was told, has not been changed since the family of the present proprietor, T.I. Malbum, took over in 1894. The tiny snugs leading into the back room are just over a century old, and their very wood breathes atmosphere.

Very good hot lunches including vegetarian dishes are served on the first floor. The second floor houses a restaurant with a more elaborate and extensive menu.

Tigh Neachtain has long attracted a theatrical and literary clientele. Hilton Edwards and Micheal MacLiammoir, founders of the Gate Theatre in Dublin, lodged here for a year in 1910, and celebrity watching continues to be a favourite pastime at the pub.

Entertainment every night with a strong emphasis on traditional music.

Gort, Co. Galway

Travelling south from Galway on N18, you reach Gort, once the dwelling place of Guaire, King of Connacht in the seventh century. The land around Gort is stitched with streams that run in and out of the rock. One such place of watery hide-and-seek is called Raftery's Cellars, after the poet.

To the north of the town is Coole Park, formerly the residence of Lady Gregory, one of the founders of the Abbey Theatre and author of the famous one-act play *The Rising of the Moon*. Coole Park was *the* rendezvous for renowned poets, writers, and artists of that turbulent and creative era from 1904 to 1916. It is now a national forest, and on a tree known as the Autograph Tree you will find initials carved by Lady Gregory's celebrated visitors: George Bernard Shaw, Sean O'Casey, Augustus John, Oliver St John Gogarty, John Masefield, and Douglas Hyde, the first President of Ireland.

Stroll through Coole Park and you will understand how its peaceful woods and lakes influenced Yeats and inspired his work: "And yet the woods at Coole . . . are so much more knitted to my thoughts that when I am dead they will have, I am persuaded, my longest visit," he wrote.

Four miles (6 km) northeast of Gort (you'll see the signs) is Thoor Ballylee. Yeats bought the tower, a square, four-story Norman keep with adjacent cottages and gardens, and restored it. In the early 1920s he summered there, and it became one of the most important symbols in the landscape of Irish literature.

Thoor Ballylee is open to the public.

Geahan's

Geahan's is the fashionable pub. There are old photos, wicker lampshades, an up-to-date jukebox, a pleasant back room, and a billiard table. The crowd consists of foreign students, local gentry, visiting intellectuals, and the usual complement of regular folk. Conversation is spirited and stimulating, and people include you more readily than is customary in the average Irish pub.

Geahan's also sponsors the Gort Poetry Contest, being well aware of the tower four miles (6 km) away that keeps the memory of W.B. Yeats forever green and the students of poetry forever arriving.

The Little Wonder Bar

Picture an evening in August. The Irish twilight is taking its beautiful time bathing the countryside in mother-of-pearl (Ireland is in the northern latitudes and in the summer twilight lasts till 11.00 p.m.). A large moon is rising over the spacious town square of Gort, and music and singing from numerous pubs mingle in the quiet air.

It is the evening of the Rose of Gort Festival. Every other house on the square is a pub, and they are all full. The Little Wonder Bar is on the corner, and inside, the ceili band (a ceili is a country dance and get-together) is playing trance music to inspire the feet of the dancers, young and old.

Some festivals in Ireland are, understandably, the creation of Bord Fáilte as a means of bringing tourist money to needy areas, but this festival seemed to be truly local; few camera toters were in sight.

The dancers stepped and twirled, children dashed about, and old men sat in a side room drinking their pints and watching TV.

Sullivan's Hotel

The other side of the square from The Little Wonder Bar is the taproom at Sullivan's.

Sullivan's is the place where the Rose of Gort contest is judged, and the lively crowd I saw was sprinkled with dressed-up young girls and boys; men in dark suits rushed around importantly.

In the bar, space had been cleared for step dancing, and two little girls were demonstrating their style, arms held straight at their sides, hair bouncing. Step dancing is popular in Ireland, and contests are held at a national level.

The band, as usual, were local men who played as a part of life instead of as a living. They played jigs and reels, hornpipes and sets with great verve. Pieces with names like "The Rocky Road to Dublin," "The Harvest Home," "Paddy Whack," "The Drop of Brandy" joined them to their eighteenth- and nineteenth-century precursors who played these same tunes. In those earlier days, dancing had become so popular that it led to the creation of a vast body of music; a conservative estimate would exceed 4,000 individual pieces.

Standing beside me at Sullivan's was the only other foreigner in view, a young Frenchman. "So nice are these musicians here," he said, "one he even gaves me his bodhrán to play and leaves me to sit into a set." He beamed at me, doubly delighted with his success at speaking English and playing Irish.

KESHCARRIGAN, CO. LEITRIM

GERTY'S CANAL STOP

This small pub features charming drawings by a local lady, a pleasant glass conservatory where you can sit and enjoy the outdoors no matter what the weather, and toasty open fires.

KILCOLGAN, CO. GALWAY

MORAN'S THE WEIR

Turn off route N18 as indicated by the small signs advertising Moran's—about twelve miles (19 km) out of the city of Galway, just south of Clarinbridge—for a real treat.

Moran's (pronounced *More*-ans) is a 200-year-old thatched cottage right beside the waters of the Kilcolgan River.

Quite simply, the oysters and salmon you eat here are the best you will ever have—anywhere. Add a few slices of home-made brown bread baked by Mrs Moran, and a pint of swarthy, creamy-headed Guinness from the tap, and you've a meal to remember.

The place is run by Willie Moran, the seventh generation to own the oyster beds that are situated at the mouth of the Kilcolgan River, part of the 700 acres (283 ha) of sea that form the Galway Bay oysterbed. Willie is a cheery host with an easy friendliness and open enthusiasm about his work.

"Hookers used to stop here on their way from Connemara," he told me as we delved into Moran's history.

Hookers? I was astonished at the vision of this healthy country spot as a port of call for Connemara girls gone-wrong.

To my relief, he went on to explain that hookers were actually heavy sailing ships built to transport turf. I also learned that during the Famine the weir, or stone wall, was constructed across the river to trap the salmon, giving Moran's its name.

Willie showed me around the old Moran homestead, now "Moran's". It was still recognisably a cottage, with its small bar and wood-burning stove where once the kitchen was, and a cosy little snug that had, appropriately, served generations of Morans as a bedroom. A dining room has been added with a pass-through bar and kitchen counter. The walls are pristine white, the floor brown tile. On the walls are many amusing photos of world luminaries who have come to this simple place. A friend tells me he once met the then-President of Ireland, Charles Haughey, over a plate of salmon at Moran's, which my friend says shows at least some expertise and sound judgment on Haughey's part.

Though 140 sides of smoked salmon and 1,000 oysters are consumed daily at the height of the season, the place always seems relaxed and congenial. In the summer, you can take your pint and sit out on the terrace watching the punters and the fishermen at work and perhaps have a plate of Mrs Moran's celestial salmon salad.

If you're having oysters, you can be assured that it's only been an hour since they were raked into baskets and minutes since they were opened. Willie is a champion shucker. At the annual Oyster Festival (14–16 September) in Clarinbridge, he opened thirty oysters in one minute thirty seconds.

This is not the only startling statistic involving Moran's: a certain Hugh Williams once devoured 158 of Galway's best in an hour and fifty minutes. Understandably perhaps, his name is illegible in the guest book.

With the advent of popularity, the Morans, displaced from their cottage, moved into a modern brick abode nearby. To an outsider, the move might seem sad, but the Morans were perfectly happy to exchange character for convenience.

Lecanvey, Co. Mayo

Lecanvey lies beside Clew Bay, a superb expanse of island-dotted sea framed by mountain ranges. Inland is a vastness of red bog broken by thin ribbons of road and dark-green lakes: Lough Mask, Lough Conn, Lough Carra.

Rearing up 2,510 feet (765 m) beside the bay is the unmistakable cone shape of Croagh Patrick. Every year, on the last Sunday in July, the mountain's solitude is broken by a national pilgrimage when thousands of people, some barefoot, climb its flanks to hear Mass celebrated on the summit. Added to the satisfaction of having done one's religious duty is the reward of a spectacular view from Croagh Patrick's crown. Thackeray rhapsodised in his *Irish Sketch Book*:

> I caught sight not only of a fine view, but of the most beautiful view I ever saw in the world . . . A miracle of beauty . . . the Bay, and the Reek, which sweeps down to the sea, and a hundred islands in it, were dressed up in gold and purple, and crimson, with the whole cloudy west in a flame."

Croagh Patrick is Ireland's "Holy Mountain," for it was here in 441 that the patron saint of the land spent the forty days of Lent in prayer for the people of Ireland.

Peggy Staunton's

This typically shabby country pub with its low ceiling, small windows, and the usual clutter of gewgaws behind the bar is a truly friendly place.

There is, in any case, something heartwarming about coming inside from the immense loneliness of the Mayo skies. Peggy Staunton adds to this sense of comforting humanity with a bright, matter-of-fact humour. Customers are lively and easy to talk to. There is also a concrete billiard room off the bar, with low windows offering the mountains a peep at the goings-on of the humans inside.

Maam, Co. Galway

Kean's Bar

Stop at Maam for refreshment beside the little bridge that fords the river. Joe Keane, who runs this nice little pub next to the petrol pump and grocery store known as Maam, tells me his pub was built in 1840 by the same Scottish engineer who built the bridge.

The interior is white-wash clean, with dark beams, a bay window, and a beautiful nineteenth-century bar. Doorways are pleasingly arched and there's a dart room for those who care to take aim. You might be lucky and arrive when there is music; no one ever knows when the musicians will show up.

Your companions at the bar will be fishermen, travellers, and shepherds, and for the first time, if you're not Irish, you may even hear Gaelic spoken unselfconsciously.

Rosses Point, Co. Sligo

> When I look at my brother's picture *Memory Harbour* - houses and anchored ships and distant lighthouse all set close together as in some old map—I recognise in the blue-coated man with the mass of white shirt the pilot I went fishing with, and I am full of disquiet and of excitement, and I am melancholy because I have not made more and better verses. I have walked on Sinbad's yellow shore and never shall another hit my fancy.

W.B. Yeats,
"Memory of Rosses Point"

All of Rosses Point was once owned by Yeats' cousins the Middletons, whose early ancestors were smugglers there. They lived in a large mansion called Elsinore, which they believed to be haunted by a window-tapping spirit. The house is still there, facing the sea in the grasslands that slope down below Ryan's Hotel.

Aussie's

Aussie's (named after Austie Gillen, the previous owner) is a 200 year old pub overlooking Sligo Bay. Visiting Aussie's is rather like exploring an attic to which all sorts of fascinating nautical paraphernalia has been relegated. The owners have always been a seafaring family, so the pub's collection of marine artifacts "just sort of happened" as a result of life rather than a decorator's scheme.

Not surprisingly, the bar menu is strong on local seafood, but also offers other choices like eggs, steaks and home-baked ham. Very tasty indeed.

Roundstone, Co. Galway

If you follow the coast road from Clifden for the fourteen miles (22.5 km) to Roundstone, you'll pass the monument to Alcock and Brown, whose pioneering trans-Atlantic flight in 1919 came to rest on a rocky hill near the town of Ballinaboy.

To enter Roundstone is to take a time-machine trip back to the nineteenth century. Beside the main road, facing the sea, is a curving row of Victorian houses, shops, pubs, and small cottages. Just north

of the town at Gorteen Bay is a two mile stretch of pure sand beach flanked by gentle dunes at one end and rock pools at the other.

O'Dowds

This pub facing the harbour is as beautifully clean and spare as a beach. You can sit on a high wooden stool and compliment your pint with delicious seafood from the bar menu: chowder, Mannin Bay oysters, crab claws in garlic, stuffed mussels, crab salad, smoked salmon pasta and an unusual salmon burger with spicy tomato sauce. Gifts from the sea are not the only offerings however — for the veggie people there are bean burgers, and for the carnivores, old favourites like shepherd's pie and steak.

Sligo, Co. Sligo

Sligo, a thriving merchants' metropolis, is northwest Ireland's most important town. It sits mostly on the south side of the River Garavogue and is encircled on three sides by mountains. That is Sligo's physical position; it is also at the centre of "Yeats Country."

Though Yeats was born in Dublin, he spent so much of his childhood in Sligo county that it became his adopted home. His stern sea captain grandfather, William Pollexfen, made his home in the town of Sligo, and on Wine Street you can still see the turret from which he swept the harbour with a telescope, checking on his ships.

Young Yeats formed his imagination around the strong impressions he received here: the beaches and mountains rich with legends; the stories told to him by country folk; the eccentricities of his varied relations — Uncle George the astrologer, who weighed his clothes before donning them; Henry Middleton, a recluse who locked his door to the world; the old servant Mary Battle, a clairvoyant. From these ingredients, the poet wove a thick web of personal and mystic imagery, an intensely Irish mythology.

Though Yeats died in 1939, he is still very much alive in Sligo. The Yeats International Summer School, held each August, is organised to service a wide range of students. There are lectures and field trips, plays and films. In the evening drinking hours the school carries on the tradition of Gaelic courts of poetry: any participant will find an audience full of goodwill and encouragement to spur him on in verse or song. (For details, write to the Yeats Society, Sligo, Co. Sligo).

The County Library and Museum has, in addition to its valuable collection of letters, photographs, and first editions of W.B. Yeats's poems, an impressive collection of paintings by his well-known brother, Jack Butler Yeats.

It is not surprising that Sligo has a fine bookshop: Keohane's in Castle Street is a treasure trove of Irish literature. After browsing here, and maybe buying a volume or two, you'll be just in the mood to repair to a good pub, of which there are several.

Beezie's

O'Connell Street

> This hostelry is dedicated to the memory of Beezie Gallagher, in reverence and respect for a truly remarkable woman.
>
> Beezie was born in the 1860s and reared on Cottage Island in Lough Gill near Sligo town. Her early years were spent as a housemaid to the Wynne family, who at that time lived in Hazelwood House, the demesne of which spread out on all sides to include Lough Gill and surrounding countryside.
>
> She later returned to spend all of her adult life on the island she loved. It was there she developed the many fascinating characteristics which make her remembered today.
>
> Being so alone and protected from society, she turned to nature for her companionship. The birds, squirrels, domestic animals and even the rodents grew to trust and love her. Jimbo McCarrick, her great friend and protector, tells of the swans sitting in her kitchen and eating from her hand, and again of her banning from the island a visitor who dared to throw a stone at a friendly rat.

Her knowledge and love of the lake was unsurpassed. Following the Great Blizzard of 1947, she returned by row-boat alone after one brief week of recuperation, having been removed from the island suffering from malnutrition — the confinement of the County Home being quite unbearable for her although she was in her early 80s.

The most endearing aspect of her personality was her natural sense of hospitality and welcome, and it is this we would most like to emulate here in O'Connell St, Sligo. The many and frequent visitors to Lough Gill would be always welcome to call, and the kettle would be boiled or the damp coat dried with the natural graciousness of the true hostess. She might then recount the famous visitors to Hazelwood House in her youth and imitate in a most talented fashion their speech and movement. Whatever the story or the circumstances of the visit the time spent with Beezie was always entertaining and the impact of her noble character guaranteed she was never forgotten.

Beezie died on the island she loved in 1951. She had visited Sligo town on Christmas Eve and had rowed out to her home from Dooney Rock nearby. When friends came to cut timber for her some days later, they found her burned to death in her island home.

With her passed another age, another time, when life was slower, nature closer and hospitality normal.

Brochure for visitors to Beezie's

Dedicated to one of Sligo's loveliest spirits, Beezie's is spacious and tasteful. From the moment the traveller steps under the green awning and enters the pleasingly Victorian ambience of palm trees, stained glass, and lamps with green glass shades, he is sure of respite from weariness.

The long front bar is partitioned in classic Irish style. The central lounge is peacefully illuminated by a large skylight, and a marble-columned fireplace with green tile adds a nice touch.

On the wall, among other things, are photos of Beezie, which make you wish you knew her, and an amusing extract from an Irish travel diary dated 1877.

HARGADON'S

OConnell Street

Hargadon's is a legendary pub in Ireland. Bought in 1868 by a

British M.P., it passed into the wise hands of the Hargadon family in 1908. Since that time, the pub's time-burnished recesses have remained unaltered, maintained in pristine and unspoiled condition. There is a pot-bellied stove, a nice old bar and wooden shelves that once held groceries.

Four snugs house the laughter and chat of the locals. Each snug has a special feature of its own: one has little glass doors on hinges that open to the barman behind the bar, another has a door giving direct access to the bar, the third has a private entry door from the street, and the fourth is extremely tiny. The whole arrangement smacks of the cosy comforts of an old-fashioned railway carriage conducive to long bouts of drink and talk; based on the sounds I heard from my seat at the bar, the inhabitants were indeed embarked on a journey of a kind.

In 1993, Hargadon's hired talented local caterers (trained by the famous cooking school, Ballymaloe House) to supply full bar food service. Dinner is served in a room at the back. Try Hargadon's pleasant garden if you like sitting outside.

McGettigan's (An Cruiscín Lan/Cruskeen Lawn)

Connolly Street

The good, country style food at excellent prices to be had here, along with a straightforwardly simple atmosphere, makes this pub a favourite for local and visitor alike.

Tobercurry, Co. Sligo

Tobercurry is a pleasant village with a golf course. If you like romantic ruins, four miles (6 km) south of town, on the Aclare road, are the remains of the fifteenth century Augustinian Abbey of Banada, beautifully placed on the banks of the Moy. You don't care about ruins but you love fishing? Ten miles (16 km) west of the village, the road skirts the northern shore of Lough Tait, stunningly situated high among the Ox Mountains. Besides being a "beauty spot," the Lough is reputed to be full of brown trout just waiting to play with you.

Killoran's

This large pub is absolutely unique in Ireland—or for that matter, anywhere. A bar/restaurant/lounge, it offers an amazing combination of entertainment, food and fun, most particularly on Thursday evenings during the summer. For only a modest cover charge, you can hear traditional music, participate in Irish dancing, try your hand at butter churning and eat. Sounds more like a country fair than a pub, doesn't it.

Unbelievably, the vittles are included in the cover price, and you'll find a very large crowd all tucking into boxty, potato cakes, crubeens and cali (the local name for champ, which is hot potato, spring onion and butter).

If you want to dig into your pocket further, you can also get organic vegetables, local goat's cheese and brown bread.

WESTPORT, CO. MAYO

Westport is the perfect town for a serious pub crawl. You don't have to worry about driving "with drink taken" because most of the town's 48 pubs are within four streets of each other, and you'll find something different and amusing in each. Of course even the most dedicated pub-ophile has her limits, so the following list and impressions are just a start for your own researches.

BLACK OAK INN

Meddlicott Street

The Black Oak Inn is comprised of several buildings on Meddlicott Street, which runs parallel to the Newport River. Originally, the river was called the Black Oak River (some say Brown Oak River), hence the pub's name. Over the years these buildings have been used as a seaweed factory, a coal company, a cement supplier, and a pub before its present incarnation as the Black Oak.

The Inn has been in the Reid family for half a century plus, and today's proprietor, the energetic, charismatic, mischievous Joe Reid, considers all of his patrons part of the family. Under his guidance, the Black Oak has burgeoned into a small fiefdom: two pubs, each with its own atmosphere, a restaurant next to the pubs, and bed and breakfast accommodation above all three.

With so much to offer, it's no wonder that the pub is a favourite with tourists and fishermen alike.

Note: if you're a darts player, be alerted—the Black Oak has one of the best teams in Mayo, with a good game available almost any time of day.

P. McCarthy's

Quay Street

The new McCarthy's opened in 1991 after being closed for ten years. The front room is all low ceilings and dark wood emitting an ambience of moody intimacy with quite a few secluded areas for small parties of six to ten people. The pièce de résistance is the dark wood, 1930s bar. The shelving behind the bar is embellished with carved posts and figures that date back to the turn of the century and were purchased at auction from a priest's house in Northern Ireland.

At the back is a large open beer garden. Tables and chairs are made from tree stumps and are set like little islands, separated by various types of foliage. The garden has its own bar outside, so service is prompt and courteous.

John McGing's

High Street

Don't walk too fast or you may miss this understated little treasure of a pub. The exterior is unremarkable and looks like a small old-fashioned grocery store—which, in actual fact, it is. The pub in the back room is more like a mini bar in someone's living room or basement; an acrylic tiled floor, an electric area heater, a small bar and a few stools, two lounge chairs, everything quite small, quite simple.

It's a plain place, but there's an aura about John McGing's, a sense of belonging, that you feel even on your first visit. People constantly pop in to buy groceries, exchanging pleasantries, little quips, knowing smiles, winks. Owner John McGing knows everyone, and as one of the oldest family run pubs in Westport, McGing's has long shared in the celebrations and tragedies of its people.

John is a treat—he knows his patrons, he knows his Westport and he knows pub laws dating back to the turn of the century, but most of all he knows how to make you comfortable. Have a pint with John. You'll be happier for the experience, and while you're there, ask him to read you "A Letter From a Kerryman's Mother." It's priceless.

The Market Bar/Hoban's

Town Square

Here we have an Art Deco bar—I mean the real thing. How did Art Deco arrive at Westport? Through St Mary's Church, that's how. Around 1920, St. Mary's was having the church floor redone in terrazzo—beige, pink and green. The church ordered too much material and the Italian workmen just couldn't stand to see it go to waste, so they used it to make the floor and counter top of the then Market Bar (the name is still in the sidewalk outside).

In 1932 Claire and Antoinette Hoban purchased the pub and re-christened it Hoban's. They elaborated on the Art Deco theme, and today nothing has really changed since their inspirations. There are fireplaces in both the front and back rooms dating from the same period. It's a jolly pub and there's even a small portable dance floor in the rear that's used quite frequently. Traditional Irish music at weekends.

Matt Molloy's

Bridge Street

In Westport the name McGing is everywhere—John McGing's Pub, the McGing Funeral Parlour, McGing, McGing, McGing. And, until May of 1989, the pub on Bridge Street was known as Dan McGing's grocery and pub, established 1896. Now however, the pub has a new name that is well-known not only in Westport, but throughout the world—Matt Molloy's. Not just any Matt Molloy mind you, but the Matt Molloy who is an extraordinary musician in his own right, as well as being a member of The Chieftains, the Irish traditional band famous the world over.

Mr Molloy has a refreshingly civilised approach to being a publican. There are no TV sets or video games in his pub, and as a sign in the front bar proclaims, "In the interest of all our patrons, no children after 9 p.m."

Matt's approach to decorating is to honour the past, but with respect and tastefulness. A shelf, built just below the ceiling, circles the walls of this former grocery store, and is filled with an array of products that were once routinely purchased at McGing's. Photos of the original store, (some with a very proud Dan standing in front) are on the walls. A blow-up of a Guinness label clearly shows Dan McGing's name printed on the bottom—a custom in the days when pubs bottled their own.

Somehow, although the pub is large, Matt has managed to convey a sense of intimacy, skilfully blending his appreciation of the past with his acknowledgment of the present. There are photos of the Chieftains everywhere interspersed with those of other musicians. Seamus Genaglety, one of the barmen, reeled off a few of the famous patrons of Matt's bar—names like Phil Coulter, Mary Black and James Galway.

Entertainment, traditional Irish music, of course, is performed either in the back room (with fireplace) or, weather permitting, in the large beer garden outside. Be prepared for a crowd, as Matt M.'s is very popular.

Tommie Nolan's

Mill Street

The easy-going, living-room atmosphere at Nolan's is probably due to the fact that the pub has been owned and run by the Nolan family for the last 80 years. Jack Nolan has been the presiding here for the last 45 of those, and what he doesn't know about Westport isn't worth knowing. Jack was born above the pub and still lives there, keeping up an old publican tradition.

ULSTER

Ardara, Co. Donegal

Donegal is the most northerly county in Ireland, stretching along much of the northwest coast. Because the country's foundation is a wild assortment of rock and stone, from cave-pocked limestone to mixtures of igneous, the scenery atop it is equally varied; sweet-smelling glens and meadows and the lushest of lush green farmland roll to the bare harshness of tumbling cliffs. Donegal offers a smiling countenance, especially in summer, bedecked with hydrangeas and wafting the perfumes of haymaking, turf smoke, and sea spray.

Ardara, prettily placed in a wide valley where the Owentocher River enters Loughros More Bay, is the place to buy your home-spun Donegal tweeds—they are made here. The town is a centre, too, for hand knitting and embroidery, all of which you can watch. Hosiery is another speciality.

To the west, Maghera Caves, Essaranks Waterfall, and the Slieve-tooey Mountains make a nice day's outing. For a good view, go six miles (9.5 km) to Loughros Point.

Nancy's

Main Street

Nancy's is an old Victorian house filled with antiques. You may find yourself enjoying a drink in the company of a small group in the sitting room; then, as more people arrive, other rooms are opened up in a seemingly endless unfolding of hospitality. Nancy's should not be missed.

Ardboe, Co. Tyrone

The High Cross at Ardboe is an excellent specimen of the more than 150 such monuments to be seen in Irish churchyards, village streets, even in open fields. Historians have long puzzled over the mystery of their haphazard distribution: clusters of them in some areas, none at all in others.

The urge to create high crosses seems to have lasted from the eighth to the twelfth centuries. They are artifacts so intricate and lacy in their stonework that a writer could be tempted to follow suit in describing them. However, I will try to control myself. Briefly: a high cross is a huge Celtic cross formed of the Christian cross with a circle surrounding the intersection of shaft and bar. An Irish friend of mine told me this represents the union of the cross and the sun, the union of Christian and pagan Ireland. It does seem like an accurate and concise way to illustrate what actually happened.

The crosses themselves were erected as monuments to victory over death—a celebration of the redemption of man by Christ. The scenes engraved on them were based on appropriate stories from the Bible, but actually they are a happy confluence of Christian symbol and pagan sensibility. The carving is alive with decorative detail: exquisitely moulded spiral patterns often enlivened by birds' heads or other animal features; complex compositions of interlacing and knotted cords; the stylised bodies and limbs of men, animals, birds, and serpents.

Irish conversation is like one of those Celtic designs

> . . . made up of a simple form like a serpent that tied itself into a thousand ornamental knots before finally eating its own tail.
>
> *Patrick McGinley,*
> *Bogmail*

The Boat Inn

After you're finished admiring the Ardboe High Cross, follow the road that goes right down to the edge of Lough Neagh until you can go no further. Now you've arrived at the lough shore area known, for reasons hidden by the mists of time, as The Battery. On this lovely spot someone had the kindness and good sense to build The Boat Inn. Although the pub itself is new, built to replace the old one which burned to the ground, the view from the bar is old as nature itself.

From your comfortable seat you can spy on herons, watch the majesty of swans and the antics of water fowl.

The Battery is an old barging stop; outside, you can stand on the quay and imagine the barges wending their way down the River Bann to Portadown, Newry, and then Dublin. It's also the site of great eel fishing and the Boat Inn is a gathering spot for the local fishermen. I was fascinated to learn that eels can be lifted out of the lake in weirs 500 stone (3,175 kg) at a time.

Appropriate reading: Seamus Heaney's *A Lough Neagh Sequence.*

Ardglass, Co. Down

This village has a fine harbour which has made it an important fishing port. Ardglass herrings are famous, and the harbour is the scene of much activity in season.

In medieval times, Ardglass was an important town and the remains of several castles are still to be seen.

The Old Commercial

This little pub is enchanting in the true sense of the word—I found myself having great difficulty leaving, a problem I seemed to share with the rest of the patrons. It is a place of pure friendliness. The antiques and decorative objects here are fascinating and have been lovingly collected by owner Ronan Fitzsimons, who also happens to be the Chief Executive for the Harbour Board Authority of Northern Ireland. Ronan spent sixteen years sailing the seas of the world for the Merchant Navy, and many of the eclectic treasures with which he returned are on view.

The pub itself is warmed not only by human kindness but more practically, by a beautiful fireplace made of Mourne granite. Behind the solid mahogany bar counter are three large stained barrels which once contained Rum, Irish and Scotch Whiskey. The magnificent low ceiling is spruce-beamed.

Ask Ronan to show you the measuring "noggins" and hydrometer in his collection.

Augher, Co. Tyrone

Jimmy Johnston's

Main Street

Here, in the Clogher Valley, you are in the heart of traditional Ulster—plain, practical, thorough, friendly—but people both North and South have heard of Jimmy Johnston's spic and span little establishment. Jimmy himself died in 1979, but the pub is tended by his sister Barbara, a trained nurse who knows very well how to take care of people and make them feel at home.

The pub is famous for its visitors' books (there were once thirteen of these, although now only three are on view), which date back to Jimmy's grandfather and earlier. As you peruse the books you'll find names that jump out at you: Hughie Green, Charles

Haughey, Monica Rose, Harry Lauder and a whole family of Charlie Chaplin offspring, for instance.

Jimmy was overjoyed when strangers from far flung lands entered his domain: an Eskimo or a Chinese person would have too valuable an address to drink otherwise than on the house. Add your name to the notables and you'll achieve a kind of fame of your own.

Next door to the bar, a shop sells delicious Augher cheese, attractively wrapped, and down the road a bit is the birthplace of William Carleton, Ireland's Dostoevsky, novelist of the horrors and humours of poverty and ignorance.

Balloo, Co. Down

Co. Down is one of the most fertile in Ireland, and the gentle, beautifully cultivated hills rise in low swells like some idyllic, half-remembered illustration from a children's book. It is also the most populous of the Ulster counties, with fine roads connecting the resorts that dot the winding coast. The county includes the part of Belfast that lies east of the River Lagan.

Balloo House

Balloo is fifteen miles (24 km) southeast of Belfast and two miles (3 km) from Sketrick Marine Centre at Whiterock, a big sailing and cruising centre, on Strangford Lough. The big Georgian converted farmhouse is a rallying centre for the huntin', fishin', sailin', motorin' crowd (the East Down staghounds sometimes meet here). The clientele is a combination composed mainly of hearty gentry and locals, and the atmosphere is boisterous and good-natured.

Ballyshannon, Co. Donegal

Sweeney's White Horse Bar/The Cellar

A pleasant pub with a fireplace in the lounge area and a good size bar. Of note are delicious home-made pies and scones. On Friday nights the place to go is down a flight of flagstone stairs and into the Cellar Bar, where the traditional music makes everyone feel euphoric. The Cellar has been painstakingly restored by the Sweeney family to its original stone beauty, with the added bonus of being comfortable.

The N15, which passes in front of Sweeney's was once the Erne River, which in 1940 was diverted west to create a hydroelectric power plant. Over the bar and at the entrance, there are photos taken when the river still ran by. You can't moor your boat at the front door any more, but there's no problem with parking your car and coming in for a pint and a session of good music.

BANGOR, CO. DOWN

JENNY WATT'S

Near the entrance to Belfast Lough is Bangor, one of the largest and best equipped seaside resorts in Ireland and one of Northern Ireland's chief yachting centres.

Bangor is a place to have a good time, which quite naturally makes it a good pub town, and Jenny Watt's is one of the most outstanding. First of all, the name of the pub is a guaranteed conversation opener. There are numerous stories and legends, all totally different, about who Jenny was and what she did to become famous. All the tales do have a common element however—Jenny always seems to wind up in a nearby cave.

As you probably have noticed, Irish publicans are great collectors and like to display their treasures as conversation pieces in their pubs. I've seen many a pub filled with odd artifacts, but Jenny Watt's really is the queen of them all. Here are displayed the most abstruse, the most unusual, the most nostalgic items; memories of bygone times, articles of clothing, of packaging, of cookware . . . you name it. Perhaps the best way to describe Jenny Watt's is to compare the pub to a time capsule.

The challenge here is to stop staring at things and exploring the place long enough to have a drink and maybe eat a little too.

BARNESMORE, CO. DONEGAL

BIDDY O'BARNES

For almost 190 years, travellers through the Barnes Gap between Ballybofey and Donegal have taken the pause that refreshes at Biddy

O'Barnes and it seems as though the very air in this pub is redolent with two centuries of talk and laughter. The pub was built circa 1800, and when you walk through the front door with its etched glass window and wrought-iron latch, the first thing that calls out to you is the commanding portrait of Biddy O'Callaghan over the fireplace.

Biddy died in 1909 at the age of 93, handing the pub down to her son John, who in turn passed it on in 1940 to Rose O'Callaghan. Rose didn't change much of anything and the slate floor, fireplace, and woodwork in the front room are original, as are many of the decorations. A rather large snug to the right of the bar was created out of Biddy's former living quarters, which now occasionally doubles as a space for dart enthusiasts.

Several years ago a modern extension was added to Biddy's, but the original building remains untouched. Wise heads realised the value and "olde worlde" charm that lies in maintaining a living tradition. The addition has ample seating, a fireplace, piano and larger bar.

Biddy's is not only a delightful watering stop for the dusty sojourner, it clearly holds a special place in local life. An announcement of an upcoming wool sale posted on the toilet doors hinted at festivities afterwards. I was sorry I had to move on down the road.

BELFAST, CO. ANTRIM

Belfast sits in its encircling ring of hills like a dark stone in a brilliant setting. To the east is the deep coastal inlet of Belfast Lough.

Sombre Victorian buildings enlivened with cherubs and reliefs of Greek gods, Indians, Chinese, and historical personages stand regally among new brick-and-glass buildings, cobbled pedestrian malls, and flowering parks. The shells of bombed and ruined houses are being rebuilt. Off in the distance, visible from almost every street, Cave Hill presents its famous profile (known locally as Napoleon's Nose).

Belfast's history is one of growth as fast and surprising as mushrooms after a rain. In the seventeenth century Belfast was a village. Then shipbuilding, seaborne commerce, linen, engineering, tobacco, and other industries resulted in the town's doubling in size every ten years.

By the end of the century the population of Belfast had grown to 2,000—a fourfold increase since 1600. The city's prosperity continued into the next century.

In 1862, Harland and Wolff was founded, a firm that was to build some of the world's largest ships. Even today, the twin cranes, "Samson" and "Goliath", of Harland and Wolff dominate the Belfast skyline. New machinery and processes also helped Belfast to a position of supremacy in the linen industry, and in the nineteenth century the population jumped from 25,000 to 300,000.

Belfast people, I discovered, have a tough wit, a lovely, caustic humour, born perhaps, from having lived with "the Troubles" for so long. Life here, they taught me, continues as it does anywhere, and a tranquil countryside lies only a half-hour bus ride away. I took a bus to the Belfast zoo one sunny Sunday afternoon. The zoo is laid out in tiers on the side of a hill, and there I found a Sunday crowd climbing around eating sweets, pushing babies' strollers, and enjoying the sights. Down below us Belfast glinted in the sun.

The following day, I set out in search of the living city, seeking what is missed by a media that reports only on sorrow. I found the exceptional Botanical Gardens, the hushed, historic rooms of the Linenhall Library, the eager talk of the students strolling the campus of Queen's University—but most of all, I discovered the heart of Belfast in her pubs.

Not only are the pubs alive and well, but Belfast has seen the revival of an exuberant and thriving night life with music, dancing and pubs of every style and size a big draw. This "revival" of the city's spirit is due partly to the emergence of what is known locally as Belfast's "Golden Mile," a burgeoning area of bistro, boulangerie and bazaar stretching from The Old Museum to Queen's University.

In Belfast, the "buzz" is all about this "Golden Mile," and I found the phenomenon akin to the flowering of the Dublin area known as Temple Bar.

The Beaten Docket

48 Great Victoria Street

Close by The Crown and Robinson's, is another Golden Milestone, The Beaten Docket. I couldn't get to the bottom of why this highly successful pub is named after a losing betting slip, but perhaps you'll have better luck.

The bar was built in 1985 on the site of the old Hamill Hotel and Adelphi Bar, in an architectural style clearly meant to fit in with the nearby Opera House: the Docket is a two storey establishment and the staircase is enclosed under a spectacular glass dome, illuminated at night.

The two levels are quite different: the ground floor is decorated in the Victorian mode. A nice detail on the beautiful mahogany bar are brass elephants holding up the rail with their trunks. Upstairs, the Hamill Lounge is a study in Art Deco with plenty of pine, Italian marble and stained ash in evidence.

THE CROWN LIQUOR SALOON

Great Victoria Street

This saloon really deserves its name — it is the crowning glory of Northern Ireland's pubs, and thought by some to be the finest example of ornate Victorian Gothic décor to be found anywhere. The Crown, owned by the National Trust and managed by Bass Ireland, is located opposite the Europa Hotel and the Grand Opera House, at the start (fittingly) of Belfast's "Golden Mile".

Established in 1826 and embellished in 1885 by skilled Italian craftsmen, the pub was given a sympathetic face-lift in 1981, when great care was taken to maintain, preserve and restore, rather than to renovate.

Even the exterior, a gift box of multi-hued tiles, coloured windows, and ornate columns gives a promise of the glories within. Inside, with the sun streaming through the stained glass windows, the atmosphere is cathedral-baroque, enhanced by a floor of intricate mosaic tiles, an elaborate ceiling of red, yellow and gold, and brocaded walls. In fact, the Crown is an ocular feast, a veritable cornucopia of detail — everywhere you look you find mirrors, etched and painted glass, fleur-de-lis, fairies, pineapples, clowns, an endless variety of amusing surprises.

The ten intricately carved snugs are in mint condition, each guarded by a mythological beast holding an armorial shield inscribed with a Latin motto such as, "Audentis Fortuna Juvat," (Fortune Favours The Brave). You can pick your own snug theme of the day.

The interior of these boxes are plushly upholstered, and you'll find everything a good Victorian gentleperson could wish for: gun-metal plates for striking matches, little windows to peep out of, and an antique bell system for summoning service.

Only the colour TV intrudes on a scene that otherwise has remained unchanged for a century.

Upstairs a more Edwardian atmosphere prevails in the Britannic Lounge, which features timbers from the S.S. Britannic, sister ship to the ill-fated Titanic.

Food: typically Irish dishes based on fresh ingredients (Irish stew, steak and kidney pie, champ) and local fish and shellfish.

Cutter's Wharf

Lockview Road

This Laganside pub has a boat-house feel to it. There's a pleasant patio beside the river, traditional jazz brunches on Sundays and a restaurant upstairs. Very popular with the University crowd.

Dempsey's Terrace & the Elbow

An "in" spot, one of the pioneers that helped begin the Golden Mile revival. The Elbow was adapted from another well-known Belfast pub, The Elbow Room, by owner Bryan West. There are three lounges in The Elbow, each with its own distinctive flavour, while downstairs in Dempsey's Terrace, you'll find five theme bars under one roof — Georgian, Edwardian, Spanish, Irish and Elizabethan. *The* late night meeting place for the over 25's.

The Dome and the Limelight

Ormeau Avenue

A music-oriented pub situated behind the BBC. Domes are the theme here: the ceiling features a rendition of the City Hall dome and several three-tiered leaded light domes. The bar was built fairly recently with great attention to fine workmanship and an eye towards creating an atmosphere similar to that of an up-market Dublin pub. Nice treatment of wood (ash) and brass.

A young crowd enjoys the Limelight disco downstairs.

The Duke of York

Royal Avenue

A much remodelled pub with traditional touches. A favourite haunt of journalists during the day and followers of traditional Irish music in the evenings.

Front Page

106 Donegall Street

Here in Belfast's old "Fleet Street" area is a laid back pub with a lot to offer: a nice "woody" atmosphere, good food upstairs, and—most especially—excellent live music: a wide range of blues, rock and Irish.

The Garrick

11 Montgomery Street

"Some bars you can walk into and it feels like coming home. Some you walk into and you feel like Spencer Tracy arriving in Black Rock on a bad day." So says journalist Billy Simpson. Billy's favourite is the two storied Garrick, which naturally falls into his first category.

The Garrick, a short walk from City Hall, has been around almost as long as the city itself. The pub is named after the world-famous actor David Garrick, who is said to have popped in for a pint whenever he was performing in Belfast in the mid-1700s.

Barney O'Neill, the pub's owner, completely redesigned the place a few years ago, restoring the panelled Victorian ceiling to its original glory, and adding a smart black and white checkerboard floor, a fine curving marble bar and a Victorian fireplace. Barney's son Bernard and daughter Paula work behind the bar and his wife Deirdre cooks the snacks for the lunchtime rush. Her bacon and egg on soda bread makes simplicity a treat.

Barney is a wonderful host and the pub draws a delightfully varied clientele reflecting his interests in golf, boxing, horse racing, and traditional jazz. Photographs on the wall show him in the company of such golfing heroes as Jack Nicklaus, Seve Ballesteros and Fred Daly, as well as jazz singer George Melly.

Kelly's Cellars

Bank Lane

Vaulted ceilings, barred windows covered with dusty cobwebs, little wooden snugs, old barrels, low whitewashed arches, glittering copper measures and a low well-scrubbed counter—Kelly's is one of Ireland's oldest bars and its downstairs section has an authentic seventeenth-century feel (the building is protected as an historic venue). Here, in the little tavern first established by Hugh Kelly in 1720, Henry Joy McCracken, United Irishman, hid under the counter from the Redcoats. And here too, the popular Joe Devlin, a member of both the British and North Irish Parliaments, once served his fellow citizens as manager of the premises.

Portraits of the pub's famous patrons over the years line the walls, yet it has lost none of the cosy ambience that made the nineteenth century novelist Hugh McCarten declare it to be like, "a sanctuary in the wilderness, a friendly inn on the mountain top."

Today's customers tend to be lawyers, journalists, and students who love the place for its atmosphere and music. Wonderful blues on Saturday nights.

Food in the downstairs bar is restricted to soup, sandwiches and perhaps a bowl of stew, but upstairs there is much more variety, including a classic Ulster Fry.

The King's Head

829 Lisburn Road

A large Victorian house has become an inspired bar, with original panelling, ceilings, mouldings and fireplaces left intact. There are a number of pleasant lounges furnished in the Victorian manner with bric-à-brac collected over the years by the owners. My own favourite room is the Victorian Library, a bibliophile's delight which still houses over 1,000 books. I was happy to learn that very few have gone missing.

A stone floored public bar and airy conservatory which easily seats 200 people, are laudable additions.

The Kitchen Bar

16 Victoria Square

The Kitchen, a traditional old pub, draws a lunch-time horde but is well worth the struggle for a table. Best tactic is simply to get there either a bit early or after the worst is over. But do go.

Before becoming a pub in 1859, the building was a boarding

house for young ladies. In its new incarnation as The Kitchen, it became the favourite watering hole of the star performers of Belfast's famous music hall The Empire. Singers, actors, clowns and dancers — all congregated here, and you can still see the theatre posters from those "good old days" on the walls of the pub.

Good pints, including real ale, exceptionally good, home-made Irish stew and pub grub.

Note: If you're interested in theatre, ask to see the box of old photos, some of them are fascinating.

LAVERY'S GIN PALACE

17 Bradbury Place

A Belfast institution, this bar is crowded by day and night, mostly with punters and students. Music and decibel count to match the customers.

MADDEN'S

Smithfield

A regular city centre pub with a reputation for good traditional music.

MORNING STAR

17 Pottinger's Entry

In a small pub in County Down I made the mistake of asking for opinions on the best bar in Belfast.

That this was naïve, I now realise. What was I thinking of—the discussion would be heated and of course no one would agree. I narrowly averted a row by ordering another round and changing the subject. The next day the name "Morning Star" was the one that remained twinkling in my mind.

As it turns out, this *is* a lovely, old, traditional pub in a listed building with a history that goes back to at least 1810. During the nineteenth century it was a favourite place for the literati and is still a splendid stop for an afterwork pint, or a refreshing pause in your travels about the city centre.

Morrison's Spirit Grocer's

21 Bedford Street

A new pub designed to recall one of those big, rambling Victorian bar-cum-general stores, once so much a feature of Ulster's country towns. Its shelves and display cabinets are packed high with glass jars, packaged goods from bygone days, icons of a long past design age.

There's simple fare at lunchtime. In the evenings, another bar upstairs keeps the same ambience, but adds music, stand-up comedy and other entertainments. Clientele: a mix of media folk and students.

Robert Stewart's Spirit Grocers

149 Ballyskea Road, Drumbeg

Records say the pub was established in 1748, but maps of the area only begin to indicate it in 1836. In any case, it is certain the place was a coaching inn on the Belfast to Dublin run and later metamorphosed into one of those pub/grocery stores where spirit, so to speak, and practical needs met.

Until thirty years ago it was a fairly notorious place with a reputation as a "man's pub" where women were barred and probably wouldn't want to go anyway.

Enter the present owner, Jackie Gilmore. Jackie, who owned several other successful pubs in and around Belfast and had his eye on Stewart's for 15 years before he was finally able to cut through a web of title complications and buy it. Once he won the pub, he poured half a million pounds into a total renovation that left the new Stewart's looking exquisitely old.

Architecturally, the pub is cottagey, with a beamed and raftered central room from which doors lead to all sorts of private and inviting nooks and snugs. Most of the old wood that is plentifully in evidence has been brought in from houses and farms all over Ireland (I sometimes think all of Ireland is being trucked from one place to another). Old photographs, farm implements, books, shoes, crockery—an odd assortment of interesting old-time artifacts—abound, but not enough to cause claustrophobia or a disease that appears to have broken out in a number of the newer pubs, an infection of the décor I have christened "Advanced, Crammed Museumitis." Instead, every detail has been thoughtfully addressed here. Even pictures and paintings, in keeping with the old-fashioned look of the place, are hung on the wall with twine.

Meals and bar food are a treat: a varied menu and good, fresh country produce prepared by a head chef with an excellent reputation. A special pastry cook is also on hand and the wine list is respectable. Stewart's has a pretty patio and tables for clear days.

ROBINSON'S

Great Victoria Street

Several years ago, Robinson's, a popular Belfast landmark and neighbour of the famed Crown Liquor Saloon, was destroyed by an IRA firebomb. It has, however, reappeared in a new and much grander guise, (following a face-lift and reconstruction job that cost £2 million) as the theme pub king of Belfast.

Robinson's, now owned by the Guinness subsidiary Croft Inns, is a complex of pubs all under one roof and set up to serve 1,670 patrons. The interior, as one commentator put it, is a "theme pub park" with four floors of bars to choose from.

For the "biker set" there is the cellar bar known as Rock Bottom with a classic Harley Davidson motorcycle mounted on a stage, a staff dressed in Harley gear, chains and motorcycle parts on the walls and appropriate music.

On the ground floor, the front bar has been painstakingly restored by a team of expert craftsmen to its former Victorian look (much of the original bar counter was salvaged), and the back bar, "Fibber McGee's" (named after a bar in New York City) has been designed to replicate a turn-of-the-century general merchant's, complete with smoked hams hanging over a turf fire.

The next level is modelled on a 1920s American speakeasy with a restaurant area featuring individual curtained snugs. The top floor bar has a balcony overlooking the speakeasy and is a warehouse style music venue.

Croft runs 11 bars, including Bob Cratchitt's at Russell Court and The Deer's Head in North Street. Robinson's is their flagship. Long may she sail.

The Rotterdam
54 Pilot Street
Down among the little alleys of the dockside, where reputedly deportees for Australia were once chained, is a bar that has real atmosphere. It also boasts a tiny garden and excellent entertainment running from pub theatre to Blues to Irish traditional music. An extremely popular place and rightly so. Affectionately known as "the Rott."

Other Dockside pubs are the Lifeboat Bar, the Liverpool Bar, Pat's.

Boho, Co. Fermanagh

McKenzie's
Seven miles (11 km) from Enniskillen is the little town of Boho famous for its caves, especially the one that supposedly goes down 200 feet (61 m) to open out into a huge cavern the size of a cathedral.

McKenzie's is a nice little pub with the main attraction being excellent music—Annie McKenzie, the owner, is herself a very fine singer of traditional songs.

Bushmills, Co. Antrim

Antrim forms the northeast corner of Ireland; on a clear day Scotland can be seen from any point on the Antrim coast. Much of the character of the county—the cottages, shops, churches, and villages—has a distinctly Scottish flavour.

The county is justly famous for a number of natural wonders; there's the twisting splendour of the Antrim Coast Road, the nine flowery glens, the miraculous Giant's Causeway (only three miles (5 km) from the little town of Bushmills). And then there's Bushmills Whiskey.

Old Bushmills Distillery

A telephone call in advance to Sheelagh Croskery at Old Bushmills—the number is 02657 31521—will reward you with a visit to the world's oldest distillery, founded 1603. Whiskey from Old Bushmills is a blend of a single malt and a single grain. In fact, the agriculture of the area is keyed to the needs of the distillery. The local barley is especially peated to the distillery's rigid specification, and the water comes from St Columb's Rill, a tributary of the adjacent River Bush. This water has a special "character" due to the fact that it rises in peaty ground and then flows over basalt.

I don't know that much about water, but here at Bushmills they are definitely doing something right, something that results in Black Bush, one of the finest whiskies in the world. After your tour of the distillery, make sure you go to the visitors' bar for a taste.

Not far from Bushmills is Dunluce Castle, which stands on an isolated crag above the sea. Its name roughly translates from the Gaelic as "Mermaid's Fort," and the waterfront tower is called Maeve Roe's Tower. The castle was the home of the MacQuillans and Maeve was their banshee. She is said to sweep the tower at night.

The Bushmills Inn

An Irish hearth, a turf fire and a welcoming rocking chair greet you as soon as you enter this tastefully restored coaching inn in view of the River Bush. The old stables have now been turned into a restaurant where you can relish your food in the intimacy of a snug of your own, or if you prefer, you can repair to the beautiful long bar in the Brasserie which is lit with Victorian gas lamps and extends all the way into the stone-flagged original kitchen.

O'Callaghan's

Musician Davey Hammond called this "a plain pub with a nice hint of shyness and reserve."

Charlie O'Callaghan is real gentleman, old-fashioned, kind and polite. Ladies are deferentially conducted to the back lounge, but with Charlie this is in no way to be construed as an anti-feminist move.

CARNLOUGH, CO. ANTRIM

LONDONDERRY ARMS

20 Harbour Road

The Antrim coast road runs 25 miles 40 km) northward from Larne to Cushendall. The drive follows the shoreline along basalt and limestone cliffs which provide entrancing views across inlets, bays and sheltering headlands. After a while there's nothing left to say except ooooh and ahhhhhh.

The Londonderry Arms hotel and bar is tucked into a small harbour and crescent-shaped beach along the way, and makes an ideal stopping point. It is highly regarded for its good, plain food available at convenient times: lunch and afternoon tea is served in the lounge and coach house (bar food and Sunday lunch in the coach house in the summer). The menu ranges from lasagne, curry and open prawn or salmon sandwiches, to chef's specials such as chicken and ham pie with chips.

Note: The building once belonged to the Churchill family and is filled with nice, old-fashioned nineteenth century furniture.

CRAWFORDSBURN, CO. DOWN

CRAWFORDSBURN INN

Along the route on the south shore of Belfast Lough, between Holywood and Bangor, lies the Crawfordsburn Inn, one of the oldest coaching respites in the British Isles. Captain Josias Bodley, who stopped here in 1603, said in his diary that he could choose from a large and beautiful cellar Muscatel wine, stuffed geese, venison pies, and various other types of game and French dishes known as kickshaws (a rough translation of *quelque chose*).

Amazingly, Crawfordsburn has survived four centuries of tempestuous Irish history. It comes complete with a majestic stone fireplace, great oak beams, stone-flagged floors, low ceilings, brandy kegs, and a magnificent seventeenth-century brass chandelier all tucked away under a thatched roof.

As you'd also expect, some of the furniture here is practically museum quality: for example a tall high-back crofter's wicker chair and a settle bed-chair with the date 1628 inscribed on it.

The Crawfordsburn is actually still an inn with 32 bedrooms, a two-tiered main restaurant and a small bistro-lounge, not to mention a much photographed, prize-winning garden.

The local drinks in those olden times were "syllabub," a mixture of sweet wine and cream; "mum," a beer brewed from wheat; and "buttered ale," beer served hot and flavoured with cinnamon and butter. The choices today at the bar are less esoteric, but probably equally satisfying.

Cushendall, Co. Antrim

Cushendall in the heart of the Glens of Antrim, is the capital of the Glens. Nearby is the sandstone Curfew Tower (once a jail), and just behind the village is Tiveragh Hill. If you're walking on the hill just at twilight and hear faint music coming from a crevice, it's either one Black Bush too many or it's the fairies who are supposed to dwell in a palace there.

McCollum's

A lovely, plain old pub with good music—songs rather than instruments.

Cushendun, Co. Antrim

Mary McBride's

Mary McBride's is one of the smallest pubs in Ireland. Actually, it's the size of a large closet, and is probably the tiniest bit of real estate to be protected by The National Trust. The legendary Mary herself died a decade ago, but her memory is still fresh to some of the bar's attendees and "Mary stories" are fun to listen to. She never drank herself and would not serve women in the bar, but if a female friend wanted a drink, she was invited into the kitchen by a side door.

Mary used to be the repository of all the gossip of the relatively isolated and beautiful valleys in the surrounding neighbourhood, and McBride's still serves as a local news exchange where everyone drops in for the latest word and a good chat and visitors are welcome for what they can report of the world outside.

Flip through the visitor's book and you'll find some famous names embedded there.

DERRY CITY

> Derry mine! My small oak grove,
> Little cell, my home, my love!
>
> *St. Colmcille*

The region from Strabane (Co. Tyrone) to Maghera (Co. Derry) is sometimes called "America's Home Counties," because it produced so many presidents, generals, and immigrants. They include General James Shields, who founded Portland, Oregon; President Ulysses S. Grant; and Charles Thomson, who drafted the American Declaration of Independence. Many country cottages in these parts have old American clocks, collector's pieces sent home long ago by emigrant sons.

The county of Derry is beautifully hilly, with a ridge of mountains, the Sperrins, rising up along the border of Tyrone and a marvellous Atlantic coastline of surf-washed beaches. Central to Derry is the city of Derry, commanding the surrounding countryside from a hill overlooking a broad tidal curve of the River Foyle.

A thousand years before the English came, Derry was founded by St Colmcille on a tree-crowned hill. Here at Doire (the oak grove) he built his favourite monastery. Since then Derry has been battled over countless times withstanding two famous sieges, which earned her the title of the "Maiden City."

Derry did not actually become a city till 1614, when a group of

London guilds provided labour and cash for the creation of the last walled city built in Europe.

The town is built on both sides of the River Foyle, four miles (6 km) upstream from the broad Atlantic inlet of Lough Foyle. Houses, churches and shops rise in tiers on the steep embankments. The Craigavon Bridge (one of the city's two bridges), is a double-decker expanse of steel that joins more than just opposite sides of the Foyle. It connects the Waterside, a largely Protestant area, to the walled city, and to the Bogside, Creggan, and Brandywell, the Catholic areas.

And bridges that connect rather than separate could well be the metaphor for what has been going on in Derry in recent times. After years of severe economic and social "troubles," the city is healing its divisions and reaching out to the world in a way that can only be described as inspiring.

From the ashes of the "Troubles," Derry citizens have beautifully revitalised and rebuilt their city centre as well as created a spectacular Heritage Centre and exhibition chronicling the story of Derry. The exhibition, housed in a rebuilt medieval fortification called the O'Doherty Tower, makes use of every form of media to tell Derry's historical tale, from diorama, film, artifacts and photographs to holograms and space age laser technology. The result, dramatically educational, serves as an unflinching yet compassionate look at the past, and a hopeful and optimistic prelude to the future.

The nearby Craft Village is just another of the success stories attributable to the Inner City Trust, a small group of people who committed themselves to create employment opportunities, involve the community in a programme of urban enhancement, and promote education and training for the young.

The brainchild of Paddy Doherty, one of the prime architects of Derry's bi-cultural renaissance, the Village combines workshops, craft shops, balconied apartments, a licensed restaurant and a delightful little coffee shop called the Boston Tea Party. There is also a fifteenth century thatched cottage called Bridie's, where Irish song and dance sessions are held at night.

As Paddy Doherty says, "This town has leaped beyond the Troubles. It's an attitude, a feeling. You sustain momentum like this by accepting that wherever you arrive, it's only a starting point."

The Anchor Inn

38 Ferryquay Street

If you enjoy the nautical, this is the pub for you. The Anchor has been done up from stem to stern to give you the grand illusion of actually being on board ship—rigging, canvas sail, captain's bridge (with small captain's cabin for intimate drinks), anchor, ship's wheel, life belt, ship's lantern, it's all there down to the last port-hole. Goofy fun.

The Bluebell

Bogside

This is the place to warm the heart of a sport's fan: a veritable picture gallery of sporting personalities and achievements are on display. Here, around a coal fire, you'll find a gathering that often includes famous names in the world of sports and good talk on the subject from boxing to football. Publican Liam Mailey is so outgoing and friendly, he'll make you feel as though he was "just only waiting for you to arrive".

The Castle Bar

26 Waterloo Street

Across the street from The Dungloe is a bar that is literally the stuff that Derry is made of. The Castle was built a century ago, using the old City Wall to form one end of the house. The person who dreamt up this idea must have been both practical and thrifty, realising that this way he'd only have to put up three walls instead of four.

Yesterday's thrift is today's treasure, and inside the pub the Wall has become a star attraction, its massive stones highlighted by concealed lighting. The pub itself is preserved from change and protected by law as a part of Derry's history.

The atmosphere is young and friendly and if you like quizzes, this pub has very good ones.

THE DUNGLOE BAR

41 Waterloo Street

"The Irish traditional and folk music that you'll hear in this pub is great," said my knowledgeable friend Stephen Doherty, "the singing and playing is the best in the Northwest." He's right, this pub doesn't just have music seven nights a week, it has supermusic. The celebration takes place upstairs, and I defy anyone to leave at the evening's end in a bad mood.

THE GLEN BAR

What can you do with two 10 ft x 10 ft rooms? Fill them with history, that's what. Specifically, railroad history. The Glen Bar has been in the Doherty family since 1907. The other occupation traditionally followed by the family has been the railroad. John Doherty, the pub's current proprietor, retired from working for the railroad in 1989 and now tends the Glen Bar full time. His father and grandfather followed the same pattern. The railroad business is definitely not just an idle fancy here.

John serves only bottled beer, but the Glen is worth the stop just for his stories about railroading—prewar stories, post war stories, great stories. And John knows how to tell them — a master raconteur.

The Glen Bar is also a bit of a celebrity hangout—John's nephew Dominic Kirwan, a country western singer and the boxer Barry McGuigan are frequent patrons. John says they particularly enjoy his truly remarkable collection of antique beer bottles.

Here in New York, I have my own antique Derry bottles to remind me of how friendly the people of that city can be. The whole thing started on a train. I was riding from Belfast to Derry and sat down next to a weedily tall boy of fourteen or so dressed in a baggy sweater and running shoes. He had to whisper because he had laryngitis, giving our conversation a comically conspiratorial flavour—I kept finding myself whispering back. After exhausting the topics of rock bands and sports, we started in on a lively discussion of Derry and pubs. He was excited by the chance to help my quest and by the time we arrived at Derry station I had a fine list of bars to investigate.

"Where are ye staying?" he asked me and I told him.

The next evening when I came home to my hotel after a long day, I was told I had a package waiting. Inside a paper bag I found two beautiful, old ceramic beer bottles glazed a two-tone light brown and grey. "Remember me and Derry. All the best, John," the note said.

THE GLUE POT/THE RIVER INN

Shipquay Street

The Glue Pot was established in 1648 and it remained a traditional pub until just a few years ago when it was renovated. Although it's been modernised, Irish imbibing history is alive and well in the pub's remarkable collection of antique stout and wine bottles, donated to the pub by hotels from all across the North. Some of the bottles date back over a century and still display very valuable labels.

The lounge downstairs is called the River End, and has recently become a video centre. It sports a large TV set and video games and because the clientele is mostly young, you'll find the sound of popular rock in the air.

THE TOWNSMAN

So ostentatious it's fun, this two-level pub is frequented mainly by the 18 to 28 year-olds. The theme is "Roman Ruins," and there are plenty of huge concrete and plaster Ionic pillars around to prove it. Upstairs, the walls bear quotations of famous Irish writers lettered in gold against a black background.

Two fires, bar food all day.

W.G'S

Society Street

After walking around the centre of the "old Derry city" you'll be ready for W.G.'s pub, just up the hill from the craft centre. Here's a pub that has remained relatively unchanged since the turn of the century. The intimate front room is the traditional, low ceilinged, nicotine-stained type of thing, and the rhythmic murmur of talk and bursts of laughter give the pub a homey, living-room atmosphere.

W.G.'s is the home away from home for a cross-section of locals many of whom are on the staff and faculty of Magee College (at one time a Presbyterian Theological College). Magee boasts one of the most extensive map collections of Derry city, many dating back to the early 1500s before the last walled city was built.

Donaghadee, Co. Down

Grace Neill's

This pub has the feel of having seen everything and it probably has. Grace Neill's is the oldest Inn in Ireland and one of the most famous. It dates back to 1611. The Grace Neill it is presently named after lived from 1818 to 1916.

Donegal, Co. Donegal

Abbey Hotel/Eas Dun Bar

The Abbey Hotel in the centre of Donegal town was opened in 1920, and the building itself dates back to the late 1700s. Although it has been totally renovated and turned into a modern facility, the ambience of the surrounding buildings and the genuine good nature of the staff give it an old world flavour, no more evident than in the Eas Dun Bar (pronounced Ash Dune Bar) where John Feely, the bar manager, will greet you with a smile, a handshake and very mischievous eyes. This is also the best stocked bar in Donegal.

While there, try a bottle of "long neck" original vintage cider—and more than likely you'll be glad you bought this book.

Draperstown, Co. Derry

The Market Inn

St Patrick Street

Draperstown is County Derry's gateway to the Sperrin Mountains, and the Market Inn is the all time favourite hostelry of writer, broadcaster, journalist Owen Kelly, a Draperstown native son.

"The Market Inn is a place where slightly surreal conversations take place constantly," he says. "My milieu is the public bar where I'll meet the man who is refusing to join the income tax scheme, or the one who knows every line Robert Service ever wrote, or the character who achieved fame of a sort by seeing little men six inches (15 cm) high dancing in the mist one morning when he was stone cold sober. The claim has never been contested but other customers wonder how he managed it when he couldn't see his cows trespassing in another farmer's corn crop.

The Market began its life as a farmers' pub back in the days of spirit grocers, but the present family, the Regans, have been keeping the fun going for the last half century. Good news often travels by word-of-mouth and apparently the word about The Market has travelled as far as Boston—it seems two members of the Kennedy clan were spotted here recently. Pictures of other celebrities line the walls.

"The Regans have always been identified with the sporting life of the community," Owen Kelly continues, "and there's a flourishing golf society based in The Market Inn. It's associated with a football team and Maurice Regan organises outings to all sorts of places for his regulars.

"Don't worry about being conscripted into any of these energetic activities if you call in for refreshments and directions. I never do. I just go for the craic in a traditional Irish pub with stools at the counter and snugs along the opposite wall. . .

"Friday is a good day for dropping in. It's market day and they serve home-cooked brown stew with a secret ingredient that's the speciality of the house. On all other days The Market Inn reverts to its ordained role in the scheme of things as a forum for the discussion of the great questions of the day, like the price of turkeys or where flies go in the wintertime."

There's a spacious lounge and a dance floor for those times when talking just isn't enough.

Drumahoe, Co. Derry

Three Mile House

Drumahoe Road

I was lucky enough to get some colourful background on Three Mile House from Sam Starrett, a local poet and historian. According to him, the building has stood at the bridge at Drumahoe for about two hundred years, beside what was once the main Londonderry to Belfast coach road. The pub overlooks the River Faughan at one of its most famous fishing spots, Clarke's Hole, known locally as The Big Hole.

In the early nineteenth century, it was a brewery and reputedly brewed 1,000 barrels of beer annually until it went out of business in 1834. The original walls of the house are still in position although there have been many alterations and additions to the building.

I was delighted to learn from Sam that the place has its own resident ghost who has been frequently heard walking about upstairs in the dead of night. The ghost has never been identified, but is thought to be the restless spirit of a previous owner, unconnected however, to a notorious murder which occurred here in 1909.

Three Mile House is now owned by Damien Villa and managed by Gary Quigley. The pub is a homey place to have a pint and the local people are more than friendly. It also has the distinction of being the only Mexican restaurant in northwest Ireland, and the food is "hot" and delicious.

Eat in the back room which has a comfy atmosphere — 2 fireplaces, private nooks and really stunning views of the River Faughan.

If you'd like to see the sights of Drumahoe with a knowledgeable and entertaining guide, ask anyone at the pub to direct you top Bob McEllhanney, a very pleasant and patient taxi driver.

Disco on Monday, Thursday, Friday and Saturday nights.

EDERNY, CO. FERMANAGH

BLACKTOWN ARMS

Devotees of traditional music can find many wonderful pubs that cater to their passion, but for those who love the old style dancing, a venue is a little more difficult to come by. Therefore, when these deprived ones arrive at the Blacktown Arms, they must feel as though they've made it into dance heaven.

Here, on a Thursday, Friday or Saturday evening you'll find that people have gathered from miles around to tread the old "heel-and-toe" and just to socialise. Here young and old, male and female, Protestant and Catholic, locals and visitors meet and dance highlands, set dances, corn rigs, kick polkas and just about all the old-time dances you can think of.

Whether you're just there to watch, or if you want to stop and catch your breath, you'll find the pub is an entertainment in itself. There are amusing things to admire, such as a display of hunting and carriage horns or set of antique dishware.

Emyvale, Co. Monaghan

Monaghan is a county formed of many small hills — as though the land were frozen waves of green and tilled fields. This is a county famous for coarse fishing and also for the clan of MacMahon, which once held sway in this territory.

Emyvale is in the heart of a magically wooded area; close by is Lough Emy, a favourite haunt for a wide variety of wild fowl and swans.

The Emyvale Inn

The Emyvale Inn is a rather small, olde worlde type of pub, decorated with horse tackle, mounted animal heads and all manner of bric-à-brac. It exudes peace and quiet and is very comfortable.

Enniskillen, Co. Fermanagh

Winding through the centre of Fermanagh is the River Erne, which expands into Upper and Lower Lough Erne, two large and fish-filled bodies of water delightfully spotted with a plethora of islands.

The county town, Enniskillen, is cleverly situated at the point where the river separates into the two lakes.

In the seventeenth century, Enniskillen was one of the principal strongholds of the English and Scottish settlers, and the centre of the corn and butter markets. Today it is noted for its handmade lace, sweaters, and china.

Blake's of the Hollow

Church Street

So named because of its position in a dip in the centre of town among a maze of time-worn buildings, this celebrated pub is thought by some to be the best in Ulster, perhaps because of its lovingly cared-for Guinness. The exterior is still painted with red and black stripes, formerly a means of identification for those who couldn't read.

Blake's breathes the very essence of a Northern county pub, where men with seamed faces gather in the light of tinted globes to sip for hours in the tranquil silence. When last I was in Blake's there was no TV to break the contemplative spell; it is switched on only for important sports events.

Coming into Blake's you leave the twentieth century behind except for automatic drink dispensers on the bottles most frequently requested, which limit the bartender's ability to pour you a friendly "stiff one." Never mind, you don't need it here anyway.

Note: To answer a question you may be tempted to pose; no, landlord Donal Blake is not related to the poet.

Glenariff Forest Park, Co. Antrim

Lara Lodge

Glenariff was described by Thackeray as "Switzerland in miniature," and he was right: waterfalls, cool ferny dells, and flowering meadows.

Lara Lodge is a rustic hostelry at the lower end of a ravishing path up the glen to a nature museum and viewpoint. Stop here for refreshment.

Hillsborough, Co. Down

Hillsborough, aptly named for obvious reasons, is the official residence of the Governor of Northern Ireland, who lives in Hillsborough Castle. There's also a fine park beside the village which features a seventeenth century fort, but for me, the star attractions of this little town are its two celebrated pubs.

The Hillside

The Hillside has a deed that was recorded in 1777, although the owner believes it to be older. The small front room lounge has stayed faithful to the pub's old-fashioned roots and has a stone-flagged floor, an Irish hearth fireplace with its old griddle, rough stone walls and traditional hunting prints. This is a lovely place to savour your pints, especially since you can buy real ale at the Hillside, and you can take your choice whether you want your Guinness at room temperature or chilled.

In a change of pace, the back room "bistro-bar" has a view over a walled garden and a more continental flavour, with a wall full of bravura modern art and interesting pieces by a local painter.

Upstairs is a restaurant with a vaulted tongue-in-groove ceiling that's a real beauty. The food is excellent, with a nicely orchestrated menu.

The Plough

Unfortunately, I can find no better word to do the Plough justice than the overworked "charming," but I can't help it—charming it is. This pub, at the top of the hill in the centre of town, should get a triple crown for food, décor and friendly and efficient service.

The deeds for the place go back to 1700 and the timbers of the front bar are even older: they were transplanted from a sixteenth century London church. As you can imagine, scenes showing beautiful draught-horses at work ploughing the fields dominate the decoration throughout the pub. You'll find not only paintings of the subject but an actual old plough share in excellent repair as well as a display case of fine old horse brasses. A large granite fireplace is lord of the lounge, and when I last heard, a conservatory was in progress which would link the front and the back of the building.

Also, as this book was going to press, the Plough was on the shortlist of six finalists for the honour of becoming UK Catering Pub Of The Year.

Holywood, Co. Down

Ned's

Holywood is the only town in Ireland to have a Maypole in its town square. Right next to this magical icon is Ned's, a time honoured, slightly spartan classic Irish pub where traditional music hits just the right note.

Killough, Co. Down

A little, old-world, fishing village of one street lined with sycamores.

Anne Boal Inn

This small, 183-year-old pub beside the sea wall has cottage style furnishings, a stone floor, a lovely big fireplace and a beamed ceiling. There are a number of interesting miniature ships on the wall including a ship's hull with a little identifying brass plate that says "Harmin Ship Building Company, 1862".

Killyleagh, Co. Down

The Dufferin Arms

On the shores of Strangford Lough, six miles (9.5 km) north of Downpatrick (St Patrick country), is a small linen town, built beside a castle. Killyleagh Castle was built in 1850 but incorporates two seventeenth century circular towers, and just in its shadow, you'll find this lively pub which is really more of an all round entertainment centre.

The business card of the owners simply refers to them as Morris and Kitty (no last names), which tells you something about their casual and warm approach. Morris and Kitty are both sophisticated world travellers, yet unpretentious and earthy as spring rain, and with a fund of amusing stories to share.

The pub is 120 years old, beautifully restored with three rooms, all with open fires. The food is hearty, Irish country kitchen fare, well prepared, and the music is a superb grab bag of everything you can think of: traditional Irish, jazz, Cajun, Blues and Soul, Folk, Bluegrass and yes, even Russian Gypsy. If you drop in you just never know what you might find, but rest assured, it will be fun.

Omagh, Co. Tyrone

McIlroy's

Music is the thing here, where tradition meets the future—excellent traditional Irish music as well as wonderful Irish progressive rock.

Portadown, Co. Armagh

Armagh is called the orchard of Ulster, for obvious reasons. A rich, fruit-growing area, it's a good place to be in blossom time. Much flax is also grown in this county, Lurgan and Portadown being important centres of the linen industry.

Nicely situated in the centre of Armagh's apple-growing country, Portadown is a railway junction for the main lines linking Dublin, Belfast, Derry, Armagh, and the North Midlands. It is also a bustling industrial centre.

The Mandeville Arms/McConville's

West Street

Among all the hustle of business, McConville's has endured unchanged, a genuine old Victorian pub in the great tradition of elaborate snugs, stained glass and rich decoration. A listed building, McConville's is like a sister ship to Belfast's famous Crown Liquor Saloon. Indeed, back when the pub was being built, the same batch of timber that went into the Titanic was used to fashion the bar. Fortunately for us, McConville's is still enjoying smooth sailing.

Portglenone, Co. Antrim

Crosskeys Inn

I was told of this pub by several Irish friends whose taste in music is impeccable and whose knowledge of same is indisputable, but when

Davey Hammond, the well-known Belfast balladeer said it was a good place for music, I was certain it had to be special.

And special it is, a Mecca for Ulster practitioners of traditional music and ballads. The owner, Eamonn Stinson, weaves a warm atmosphere and welcomes converts to the eloquence of Irish music.

The setting for the music is perfect—an old country pub (once a coaching stop), with thatched roof and turf fires, situated near Lough Neagh and the broad River Bann.

Lough Neagh harbours many legends, as does almost every part of the Irish landscape. Beneath its waters, which reputedly can turn wood into stone, there is said to lie a town. The magic lake was created, goes the story, when the giant Finn MacCool grabbed two handfuls of earth to fling at an enemy. The place where he dug filled up and became Lough Neagh, and the two fistfuls of earth became the Isle of Man.

> On Lough Neagh's banks as the fisherman strays,
> In the clear cool eve declining,
> He sees the round towers of other days
> In the waves beneath him shining . . .
>
> *Thomas Moore*

PORTRUSH, CO. ANTRIM

If you like the combination of a golf and seaside resort, you'll love this little town. Portrush, situated on a dramatic promontory ending to the north in Ramore Head, offers two 18 hole golf courses (including the Royal Portrush championship course), and a nine hole pitch and putt course. When you've finished your game, you still have a stunning beach, tennis courts, bowling greens, swimming pools, boating and fishing to amuse you.

THE HARBOUR BAR

There are certain pubs that I found were repeatedly recommended to me as being exceptional. The Harbour Bar is one of these. Why? Because, among other things and according to popular opinion, it serves the best Guinness in the North.

Choose among a delightful warren of cosy little rooms still structurally much the same as when the pub opened in 1836.

Portstewart, Co. Derry

Portstewart is a place for holidays. There are pools and coves and surf-washed sands that stretch nearly two miles from the cliffs south of the town. There are two 18-hole golf courses, tennis, boating, and sea fishing.

The Anchor

Just go, all right? If you don't think it's a really special pub, write and tell me why I'm wrong.

O'Malley's

The Edgewater Hotel

Although the hotel is only a half century old, it gives the impression of being an aged rural inn. Its bar faces off the tiny wood-panelled lobby toward a view of the magnificent ocean beach between the town and the River Bann. It's a favourite retreat for fishermen fresh from angling for sea bass, sea trout, porbeagle sharks, and tope.

Ramelton, Co. Donegal

Conway's

A thatched roof, a nice little old bar with a high counter, and attractive country fixtures make this a good place to linger for a while. Notice the American pendulum clock. At the turn of the century, when somebody from the countryside emigrated to America, practically the first thing they'd send home would be a clock, because in those days not too many country families owned one.

These "American" clocks are really charming; they're obviously mass produced, usually made of a simple wood like pine and decorated with bits of carved curlicues and fretwork and a little printed pastoral scene. The clockmaker would sign the piece with his name and the American town it was made in. They're cheap, cheerful clocks and look as though they came from a fairground, and of course now they've become collector's items.

Rathmullan, Co. Donegal

Rathmullan is the kind of old-fashioned resort you associate with tea in ancient sea-front hotels, with sand castles, beach umbrellas, and rolled-up trouser legs. It is situated on the shores of Lough Swilly, a fjord-like arm of the sea that reaches inland for 25 miles (40 km). Rathmullan's strand is blessed with a series of sandy coves, like exclusive little stone-walled rooms, each with its own private portion of land and sea.

In the eighteenth century, Rathmullan was the headquarters for England's North Atlantic fleet. They built the pier that still serves the town today, and left behind a wrecked ship (said to have carried bullion) at the mouth of the lough — to the fascination of several generations of Rathmullan boys.

In the 1920s Rathmullan was a major fishing port where Russians came to buy the barrels of salted North Sea herring, and where buyers came from Cyprus and the Canaries to purchase Donegal seed potatoes, still considered to be Ireland's best.

The Pier Hotel

The Pier Hotel has sheltered its share of this colourful crowd of visitors. James Deeney, the proprietor, is the third generation to welcome strangers to the pier, and surely, of his five children, one will continue the tradition of friendly conversation and well-pulled pints. Steaks are good here, too.

For a special treat, try dinner at Rathmullan House, the former residence of a well-to-do Belfast family now famous for its spectacular elegance, gardens, and food.

Strabane, Co. Tyrone

The Blue Palate

The Blue Palate, which is owned by Punjabi people, happily marries Indian management with Irish tradition. The music here is very fine — Irish traditional and progressive Irish rock.

Warrenpoint, Co. Down

Aylesfort House Inn

Here's a way for you to take a drink and go to church at the same time. The Aylesfort Inn, situated at the edge of the busy little harbour town on the north shore of Carlingford Lough, is completely outfitted with what were once the contents of a lovely old church in the English town of Aylesfort in Kent.

Here are pew ends on the seats, mahogany altar railings round the snugs, wooden Gothic arch designs on the front of the bar, oak panelling round the walls, exquisite stained glass work, and overlooking all, the imposing central pulpit.

Frank O'Hare, the publican, jokes that when he first opened the Aylesfort this was the only way he could get a Sunday drink licence. The locals tell how one of their number set out each Sunday evening in his best church-going suit and was able in all good conscience on his return to tell his wife that he had been sitting right below the pulpit.

In the ceiling of the public bar is a spectacular stained glass window which is attributable to another sort of temple — it was originally the pride and joy of the Allied Irish Bank (now First Trust) in Armagh.

The Aylesfort is a three level pub and the restaurant and nightclub on the upper floors combine plush comfort with a kind of glamorous glitz.

The Parting Glass

All the money e'er I had
I spent it in good company;
And all the harm I've ever done,
Alas! It was to none but me.
And all I've done for want of wit
To memory now I can't recall:
So fill to me the parting glass,
Good night and joy be with you all!

If I had money enough to spend
And leisure time to sit awhile,
there is a fair maid in this town
That sorely has my heart beguiled.
Her rosy cheeks and ruby lips
I own she has my heart in thrall
Then fill to me the parting glass
Good night and joy be with you all!

Oh, all the comrades e'er I had,
they're sorry for my going away;
And all the sweethearts I e'er had

They'd wish me one more day to stay,
But since it falls unto my lot
That I should rise and you should not,
I gently rise and softly call —
Good night and joy be with you all.

Traditional ballad

Index to Cities and Towns

Index to Pubs